simple fountains

for indoors & outdoors

simple fountains

for indoors & outdoors

20

step-by-step

projects

DORCAS ADKINS

STOREY BOOKS

Schoolhouse Road
Pownal, Vermont 05261

The mission of Storey Communications is to serve our customers by publishing practical information that encourages personal independence in harmony with the environment.

Edited by Deborah Balmuth and Nancy W. Ringer
Cover design by Mark Tomasi
Cover and all interior photos by Giles Prett except those by David Egan (Hampstead, Maryland) on page 112;
Maggie Oster on pages 48, 51, 54, 64, 66, 88, 90, 95, 101, 114, 117, 120, 123, 126, 130, and 138; Jerry Pavia
on pages 6 and 44; Bob Romar/cfp photography for Maryland Aquatic Nurseries on pages 22, 26, and 27;
and Sabine Vollmer von Falken on page 78
Bowl on pages 16 and 21 by Constance Talbot, High Hollow Pottery, Windsor, MA 01270
Text design and production by Mark Tomasi
Line drawings by Terry Dovaston
Indexed by Susan Olason, Indexes & Knowledge Maps

Printed in Hong Kong by Regent Publishing Services
10 9 8 7 6 5 4 3 2

Library of Congress Cataloging-in-Publication Data

Adkins, Dorcas
     Simple fountains for indoors and outdoors : 20 step-by-step projects / Dorcas Adkins.
         p.   cm.
     Includes index.
     ISBN 1-58017-190-7 (alk. paper)
     1. Fountains—Design and construction.   2. Water in landscape architecture.   I. Title.
TH4977.A33 1999
731.72—dc21   99-18137
                                                        CIP

Dedication

I dedicate this book to my parents.

When I was a child, I thought that they could make anything.

When I was a teenager, I thought that if they could make it, anybody could.

Now that my own children are grown, I appreciate more than ever the gift

my parents have given to all of us — a love for making things.

Acknowledgments

This book is the result of my past decade of partnership with Bob Adams. When he built our first portable fountain-pond nobody had ever seen anything like it. We found ourselves meeting a growing demand for this new necessity and have responded with the steady stream of new designs we currently produce and market worldwide. Without Bob's vision and energy, this book would have been very different.

Pat Muñoz, by teaching me to kayak, has shown me more falling water in more breathtaking settings than I could have believed possible. Additionally, she has given her words of encouragement and her hours of editorial patience to the work itself.

Deborah Balmuth, Nancy Ringer, Giles Prett, and Mark Tomasi of Storey Books, with their good humor and willingness to work hard, have shown me that it takes a village to make a book.

Contents

Introduction

Of all nature's elements, water is perhaps the most essential to life, health, and happiness. For many species of plants and animals, falling water provides increased oxygen. This all-important ingredient combines with carbon, enabling waste from these organisms to decompose quickly. For aquatic animals such as fish, snails, and crayfish, adequate dissolved oxygen in the water is required for life itself.

Since the earliest times, we humans have acknowledged the vital importance of water in our lives. Our bodies are made up mostly of water, and without sufficient water to drink or to humidify the air around us, we quickly become uncomfortable.

When water is in motion, it humidifies the surrounding air more readily. It also produces sounds that relax us. Nothing smoothes the furrowed brow like the soft lap of wavelets on a lakeshore, the thunder of surf on a barrier island, or the silvery tinkle of a stream falling through the spring forest.

The Sound of Moving Water

Modern life is very busy. Technological advances have resulted in a world where sensory overload is common. Many of us recognize that the only antidote is frequent communion with natural forces, yet too often we cannot spare the time to go into the wild to find the peace and relaxation we need. Instead, we create increasingly elaborate garden refuges for this purpose. For many reasons, not the least of which is that the splash of falling water can be used to mask traffic sounds, fountains enhance these gardens, both indoors and out.

The indoor fountain can provide the melodic sound of falling water in the workplace. By setting this piece of the outdoors beside your computer, you can add humidity to air often dried by heaters and monitor fans. The release of negative ions that takes place in falling water is thought by many to soothe the human spirit as well.

In the outdoor garden nothing could be more natural than the inclusion of a water feature. Even the most formal fountain — one in which the water decorates an elaborate sculpture and falls into a pool scoured clean of life forms — contributes cooling humidity to the garden environment while masking the noise of the street. A more natural fountain bubbling into a pond full of fish, frogs, snails, and water lilies quickly becomes a successful and sustainable ecosystem. The lessons we all can learn in such a classroom are invaluable as we face the challenges of sustaining our own planet's environment into a complex and crowded future.

Modern Fountain Design

The convenience of the electric pump, recently developed in tiny yet reliable models, allows all of us to easily create small fountains for our own gardens. The style we choose for a water feature can range from a formal pool, soothingly geometric in form, to a natural mountain cataract. Or a spare and simple Zen garden, complete with koi pond and bridge, can appear in what was once an unused alley.

And the same small pumps allow us to bring our love of water into the inner spaces of our homes. Beside the computer station, where quiet is interrupted by only the occasional chirp and whir, the chuckle and burble of a bowlful of stones can be clearly heard.

In this book I hope to encourage you to make your own fountains. I offer a wide selection of projects

Feng Shui

The ancient Chinese art of placement, called *feng shui,* has long used fountains to place water in key locations within the home and garden. According to the principles of *feng shui,* water attracts the all-important *chi,* or energy. *Chi* manifests itself as "wealth" — not just in money but in health, happiness, love, and general good fortune as well. Placing a fountain in the entryway of your house, then, can have benefits on many levels. Not only does this piece of water art decorate a space often in need of added interest, but it also attracts *chi* through the front door and into the home. As appreciation of *feng shui* expands worldwide, more and more of us are using water in our living spaces.

employing as many of the materials suitable for use with running water as possible. Some can be constructed using recycled objects and your own hands. Most require that you have access to tools. By reading the introduction to each project, you can determine whether its procedures are within your reach.

Each individual fountain project I include here has step-by-step directions — but I offer these only as a guide or starting point. I encourage you to browse these chapters, go buy a pump, and plunge right in. Combine elements of different fountains, simplify, and improve on the suggested steps. Remember, that you can fix nearly anything by doing it over again; relax and dare to make the all-important mistakes. No written description has the power of hands-on trial and error to give you the confidence and joy of making your own operating piece of water art.

Designing your own fountain will add immeasurably to your enjoyment of it. The lessons we can learn from water, the master, are many. On the one hand, it's a very forgiving medium; if you're sensible, the worst thing that can happen is that you find yourself mopping up the floor. On the other hand, water is a formidable force. It can, and sooner or later will, find its way into every crevice, move the earth, and break down mountains. Working with water teaches respect, even to the respectful. It demands discipline, patience, and focus.

This simple yet elegant design for a small tabletop fountain is constructed almost entirely of copper. The water drips down from the top of the arcing pipe, slides down the slowly spinning copper tail, and is gently flung into the reservoir.

Still, as you work to contain water and use it for your purposes, the scattered interruptions of your day will fade into the background. You'll become completely present in your work.

It is my hope that this book will get you started. Buy a pump and begin to play with it. Try out your own fountain designs. Make mistakes. Most importantly, have fun.

1 Materials and Supplies

A fountain is by nature an illusion. You, the fountain maker, strive to emulate nature and to conceal the machinery that makes the illusion possible. You build an image of a credible natural water source, flowing downhill through your garden, perpetually pouring from a moss-covered clay jar in an indoor tabletop fountain, or spilling from a bamboo spout spiked at the top of a wellhead.

There is an infinite variety of materials and supplies you could select for your fountain project. The constant recirculation of water that creates a fountain requires only a few basic parts to function; the type of part you choose, and how you arrange all the parts together, is a uniquely personal journey.

Getting Down to Basics

No matter how small or large your fountain is, it will consist of a few basic elements: the reservoir, the pump, and the fountain piece.

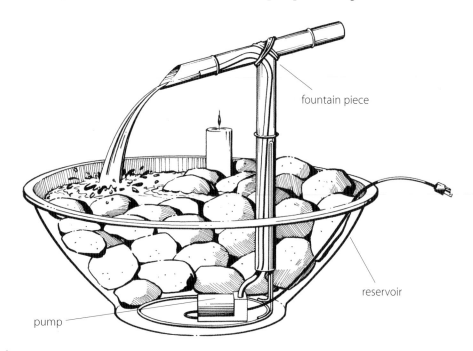

All fountains are composed of three basic parts: the reservoir, the pump, and the fountain piece.

pumps keep water constantly recirculating through the system, fountains are not wasteful of water. Only that lost through evaporation must be replaced, and the humidity this provides benefits both plants and animals that live nearby. Most fountains are powered by small pumps submerged in the reservoir, from which the pumps draw water into their *housings*, or outside shells, through some sort of intake. From there the water passes through the body of the pump, where it is driven by an *impeller,* a water propeller spun by electricity that forces the water from the pump's outflow fitting. Most small fountain pumps have a *flow control* to regulate this outflow of water.

The *fountain piece* is the waterfall, sculpture, or spout from which the water falls into the reservoir. Plastic or copper tubing is often used to carry the water from the pump's outflow fitting to the highest point in the fountain piece, from which it falls.

Water gardening and fountain making are gaining enormous popularity. Most good garden centers and even home centers these days carry a selection of all the necessary materials, including pumps, fountain attachments for pumps, pool liners, and preformed pools. Several mail-order suppliers are listed in appendix C (page 147).

Location, Location, Location

Before you begin to design your fountain, consider its eventual location. If it is to be used indoors, will you place it on the floor or on a table or desk? If on the floor, be sure your flooring material is water-safe (stone, tile, linoleum), since even the most careful fountain maker will spill water occasionally, and accidents will happen. On a table or desk, be sure the finish can tolerate some moisture.

Location may also dictate the size of the fountain. An outdoor waterfall needs to be large enough to be heard from outdoor living spaces nearby. This requires a relatively large pond and pump. Conversely, the indoor fountain needs to be tidy in operation. Splashing is very destructive and can quickly create a water-damaged zone around the

The *reservoir* is the part of the fountain in which water is collected and stored, and from which water is drawn. It usually contains the pump and fountain element. It can be as large as a pond or as small as a serving dish from your cupboard. If it's to be used indoors, it must be watertight. Outdoors, some leakage can be tolerated.

Pumps run on electricity, either solar- or house-powered, and allow you to enjoy a steady stream of water. Because

fountain. Choose an indoor pump of small size and with variable flow to prevent splashing.

Choosing a Reservoir

Your fountain's reservoir will collect and store water, as well as contain the pump and fountain element. In a large outdoor fountain, the reservoir may be a pond or large container. In a small indoor fountain, the reservoir must be watertight and deep enough to allow you to conceal the pump, and must

hold enough water so that the pump doesn't run dry too fast. Many materials are suitable for fountain reservoirs.

Wood. Beautiful and relatively easy to cut and join, but in most applications, must be protected from water. For outdoor fountains, where initial leaking will do no harm, you might want to fill a half barrel with water and allow it to swell, producing a nearly watertight container that will last for years. Indoors, you can apply fiberglass or plastic laminate directly to wood, line a wooden reservoir with a piece

of flexible rubber *pond liner* (a sheet of plastic or rubber specifically made for use in waterproofing ponds), or build a wooden *surround* (a frame of wood) around a copper liner or a rigid plastic tub.

Concrete. A porous material that will always sweat slightly, but is easily molded and produces a pleasantly rustic surface.

Metal. An antique pan or trough of copper, tin, or lead makes a beautiful, practical reservoir. Any leaks can be patched with silicone caulk.

Ceramic. Fashion your own large stoneware bowl, or find one for sale at a craft fair, in a secondhand shop, or in an import craft shop. Be sure to test all pottery for watertightness. If you find that it "sweats" moisture, coat it with silicone caulk or concrete waterproofing solution.

Ceramic tile. Watertight when thoroughly bedded in tile adhesive or silicone caulked onto a rigid surface. The almost unlimited range of tile available allows you to create a stunning fountain.

Resin. A catalyzed material poured into molds to create a huge variety of shapes. With the introduction of stone or bronze dust, resin can approximate the surface qualities of these materials.

Reservoirs come in a variety of sizes and materials. The eventual location of your fountain, including the atmosphere you want to create, will determine the appropriate reservoir for your project.

Many garden centers sell large resin bowls for planting. They're watertight, and can be worked easily with a drill or router to create such features as a cord notch.

The Pump and Electrical System

The pump is the heart of every fountain. Until recently all pumps were of the "direct-drive" style. Here, the motor is encased in an oil-filled waterproof shell with seals around the cord and impeller shaft. The usual size and output power of direct-drive pumps made small indoor or garden fountains difficult to construct.

Lately, however, very small tabletop fountains have become possible through the introduction of the magnet-driven ("mag-drive") motor. In this case the impeller is attached to a magnet that twirls in a chamber outside the epoxy-sealed pump housing. The chief advantage of this design is that the wiring is sealed off from the moving parts. Water and electricity are kept apart by a solid plastic wall. Far less bulky than direct-drive models, mag-drive results in smaller pumps. It is significant, too, that epoxy, a solid and inert material, cannot leak from the housing — as can the oil from a direct-drive pump. I have seen this happen in my own pond. Imagine how fast you must move to contain such a miniature ecological disaster!

Most small plastic pumps are of the mag-drive type. These pumps are less powerful than direct-drive pumps (sometimes an advantage in small fountains) but more prone to jamming. Not only is there a whirling impeller to jam whenever a bit of leaf or twig finds its way past the intake screen, but there is also a cylindrical magnet spinning in a well where silt-laden water is circulating. Even the crumbs of calcium carbonate formed by the evaporation of hard water can jam the magnet. This sensitivity to jamming may limit the use of mag-drive pumps to cleaner, indoor applications.

The pump often turns out to be the most expensive component of the fountain, ranging in cost from $30 to $100. Cost can serve as an indicator of performance, as pumps of comparable quality and power usually cost about the same amount. The less expensive aquarium pumps will work in small fountains but rarely have the flow control mechanisms that allow you to adjust waterflow. If you want to use an aquarium pump but it's forcing water too powerfully, you can try to restrict waterflow by placing a hose clamp on the tubing that carries water to the pump.

Size, Intake, and Outflow

Choosing a pump for a small tabletop fountain involves different concerns than for an outdoor water feature. The most important one is output. Generally, your challenge will be to find a pump that will deliver a small-enough flow of

water, since splashing is destructive to surrounding furniture.

Consider also the physical size and shape of the pump housing. Ideally, this will be completely concealed when your fountain is assembled. When choosing your pump, imagine it in the fountain you will construct. Is the outflow on the top of the pump or on the side? Will this matter in your fountain? Is the water intake on the bottom or on the side? If you need to orient the pump so that the intake is on the pump's side, will the depth of the water reservoir allow this intake surface to be completely covered? (This is necessary for the pump to draw water.)

Most tiny pumps come with suction-cup feet to help hold them in place. Because the pumps weigh very little and are attached to relatively stiff tubing and

This small mag-drive pump is the perfect size for a tabletop fountain.

electric cords, this can be an asset. Often, however, the design of your fountain will dictate a different orientation than the feet suggest. Don't worry about whether your pump will sit on its feet or lie on its side as long as there is plenty of water covering the intake surface.

Choosing the Right Power

Pumps are differentiated by volume. Usually, a small portable fountain will use a submersible pump with a volume of between 60 and 140 gallons per hour, or GPH (217 and 532 l per hour). Although you can use this rating to make your initial selection, nothing works as well as actually field-testing the pump in the fountain you are constructing. Be sure to keep your receipt and packaging in case you need to return the unit.

If you're creating a large outdoor fountain, you'll have plenty of room to accommodate your pump. But will that pump have sufficient power to lift water to the top of your waterfall? To calculate this, the following rule of thumb is often used:

For each inch (25 cm) of stream width at the top of the fountain piece, choose a pump that will deliver 100 gallons (380 l) per hour (GPH) at the height of the overflow point (known in the trade as "the head"). For example, let's say that a waterfall begins at a point 3 feet higher than the surface of a pond, and that the streambed is 5 inches wide at the point of overflow (top). Your pump supplier can tell you how many gallons per hour (GPH) each model delivers at different heights above the pond's surface (feet of head).

Select a pump that delivers at least 500 GPH (1,900 l per hour) at 3 feet (90 cm) of head.

Flow Control

When selecting your pump, look for the flow-control mechanism. Be sure it operates smoothly and has a variable range. This is an integral part of a small pump for an indoor fountain and will be very important for eliminating splash.

For a large outdoor fountain, you can buy a flow-control valve and add it to the tubing between the pump and the fountain element. This will eliminate the need for flow control on the pump itself, which is often inaccessible once you set up the fountain.

Pump Noise

There is no such thing as a soundless pump. Any electrical device emits at least a soft hum when operating. Some pumps are quieter than others, and some fountains, usually those with the pump submerged in deeper water, conceal the sound better than others. I've found that the small magnet-driven fountain pumps are relatively quiet, whereas some inexpensive aquarium pumps have proved noisy and impossible to adjust.

Housing Material

In the larger direct-drive pumps you are sometimes presented with a choice among plastic, aluminum, steel, and brass for the housing material. Here the issue to consider is that each material will erode to some degree in the water.

Chlorine and salt attack aluminum, as does the ammonia in fish waste. Plastic is attacked by the ultraviolet rays in sunlight, shortening its life in outdoor situations. The added investment in stainless steel may be worth your money. And remember that whenever you are selecting a large pump for an outdoor pond or waterfall, it is wise to take advantage of the free advice most retailers are eager to provide.

GFCI Outlet

Every fountain pump, whether indoors or outdoors, should be attached to a ground fault circuit interrupter (GFCI). The GFCI immediately breaks the circuit when it senses a short circuit or other damage to the wiring attached to it. This can prevent shocks from pond water charged with house current should the cord to your pump be accidentally cut. Almost all building codes now require GFCIs on any circuit installed in a potentially wet location such as a bathroom, kitchen, or pool area. You can tell if you have one because you'll find a red reset button on the outlet itself. If you don't have a GFCI outlet, you can purchase one that will fit over an existing outlet; for an outside water feature, you can buy outdoor extension cords complete with circuit interrupters included on the plug. Run this cord through a buried pipe wherever foot traffic or other hazards threaten its safety.

The water hyacinth, sometimes known as "the sewage treatment plant," grows quickly, producing beautiful showy purple flowers in full sun. It's a tropical plant and will be killed by frost. In climates where there is no frost, however, it has become a serious pest in waterways and must be kept from escaping into the wild.

Filters

The small indoor fountain pump often comes with a built-in foam sponge filter. Although these often fill quickly with mud and require frequent removal and cleaning, they may keep bits of mud and plant material away from the impeller and its chamber. If your pump comes with one and it deteriorates over time, or if you lose patience for cleaning it, you may safely run the pump without it as long as there is a grill over the pump's intake to keep larger material from jamming the moving parts. In outdoor ponds where fish waste and decaying plant material accumulate, filters can be necessary.

Biological Filters

There are almost as many designs for filters as there are water gardeners. The most ingenious are sometimes the simplest. Richard Schuck of Maryland Aquatic Gardens proposes a biological filter using what he terms "the ten percent solution." He makes a smaller pond above his main pond. The small pond has an area roughly 10 percent that of the main pond and is thickly planted with water hyacinths. Water is pumped from the main pond into this biological filter, where it is very effectively purified as it passes through the dense mat of plant roots and then spills back into the main pond. Schuck says

the water in his large pond cleared in just a few days with this treatment.

For a more compact style of biofilter, see Barney Webster's lava rock and tub assembly in chapter 5. This style is especially suited to the small reservoirs found in many outdoor fountain pools where fish waste needs to be removed from the water.

The Fountain Piece

In every fountain the key design element is the apparent water source. Generally, the true water source is the pump and the piece of vinyl hose from which the water gushes. How you choose to disguise this fact is the key to the creation of your fountain.

Many garden centers and hardware stores sell pumps that come with a selection of fountainheads ready for attachment. If you have a pond or other water reservoir large enough to contain the splash these usually create, you can set one of these in place, plug it in, and enjoy the small hydrodynamic show immediately. However, you can also choose to make your own fountain piece from a variety of materials:

• Stacks of natural objects, such as stones, driftwood, shells, or pottery pieces — when the pump and hose are concealed, the water seems magically to pour from this assembly

• Old tools and containers such as watering cans, clay jars, and the iron pumps used on wellheads

• Cylindrical spouts fashioned from bamboo or soldered copper pipe

• Carved pieces of durable yet malleable material, such as lava rock or rot-resistant wood

• Sculpture pieces, purchased or handmade

Connecting the Pump to the Fountain Piece

In order to get water from the pump's outflow to the "mouth" of your fountain piece, you'll need some extension vinyl tubing, available at most hardware, gardening, and craft stores. You may find that the ideal size (in terms of diameter) of hose for the mouth of your fountain is different from the size you need to fit over the outflow fitting on your pump. If this is the case, you can "telescope" together a series of incrementally smaller sizes to make the transition.

Definitions

Inside Diameter: The measurement of diameter across a cross-section of tubing from inside its walls; often abbreviated as **ID.**

Outside Diameter: The measurement of diameter across a cross-section of tubing from outside its walls; often abbreviated as **OD.**

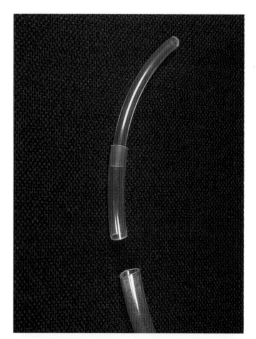

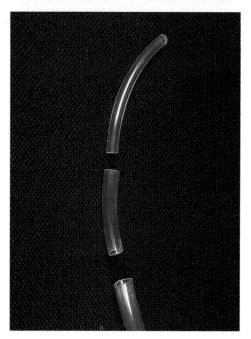

If your fountain piece is sized for tubing of a particular diameter, and your pump outflow is sized for tubing of a different diameter, you can telescope together incrementally smaller pieces of tubing to make the transition.

Vinyl hose comes in increments of ⅛ inch (3 mm) in inside diameter (ID), and has a fairly consistent wall thickness of about 1/16 inch (1.5 mm). The incrementally next-bigger size, then, will usually fit snugly over the size you have in hand.

Since hose is not expensive, it's a good idea to buy a few feet of several consecutive sizes. You can easily trim it to size with a sharp kitchen knife or a pair of scissors.

Where Can I Find ...

One of the most common questions in any creative building project is "Where can I find that?" Here's a quick answer, addressing the most common fountain-making materials.

Some of the most unique, beautiful decorative pieces to add to fountains can be collected at the seaside.

Material	Use	Where Available
Antique tubs (metal and stone)	Reservoir	Farms; flea markets
Bamboo	Fountain element	Mail-order catalogs; garden centers; your backyard
Biofilters	Pump attachment	Pond supply companies
Casting plaster	Moldmaking	Home and building stores
Cedar fencing boards	Reservoir surround	Home and building supply stores
Ceramic bowls	Reservoir	Garden centers; home supply and import stores
Clay	To build fountain elements or reservoirs	Art and ceramic supply stores
Clay modeling tools	Working with clay	Art and ceramic supply stores
Concrete garden sculpture	Fountain element	Garden centers; home supply and import stores
Concrete mix, sand, gravel	Making reservoir or fountain element	Home and building supply stores
Concrete planters	Reservoir	Garden centers; home supply and import stores
Concrete tubs	Reservoir	Garden centers; home supply and import stores
Copper tubing, rigid and soft	To carry water through fountain system, or use as fountain spout	Garden centers; home supply stores
Epoxy and silicone caulk	Sealing and waterproofing	Home and building supply stores
Epoxy putty	Waterproofing	Home and building supply stores
Filters	Pump attachments	Pond supply companies
Glass aquariums	Reservoir	Pet stores
Glass bowls	Reservoir	Import stores
Grout	Filler between ceramic tiles or mosaic pieces	Home and building supply stores
Lava rock	Fountain element	Garden centers and landscape stone companies
Mastic	Tile adhesive	Home and building supply stores

Material	Use	Where Available
Metal planters	Reservoir	Garden centers; home supply and import stores
Muriatic acid	Ingredient in metal patina solution	Home and building supply stores
Patina solution	"Antiquing" soft metals	Craft stores
Plastic laminate	Sandcasting mold material, waterproof liner for reservoirs	Building supply stores
Plywood	Base of fountains and reservoirs	Home and building supply stores
Polyester resin	Waterproof sealer for reservoirs	Building supply stores and marine supply companies
Polyester resin bowls	Reservoirs	Garden centers; craft stores; florists
Pond liners	To create an in-ground reservoir, or line reservoirs that are not waterproof	Garden centers; pond supply companies
Pumps	Provide power to circulate water	Garden centers; pond supply companies
Re-bar	Concrete-reinforcing rod used as a support for standing fountain elements	Building supply stores
Romex wire	Support for standing fountain elements	Building and electrical supply stores
Sheet copper	Raw material for reservoir	Building supply stores
Soldering tools, flux, solder	Working with copper	Garden centers; home supply and import stores
Spray wax	Moldmaking	Home and building supply stores
Tile scorer and nipper	Cutting ceramic tiles	Home and building supply stores
Vinyl hose	To carry water through fountain system	Garden centers; home supply and import stores
Wooden barrels	Reservoir	Garden centers; home supply and import stores
Wooden troughs	Reservoir	Farms and garden centers; make your own

2 Tabletop Fountains

The dainty streams of tabletop fountains murmur and chuckle in our most intimate living spaces. With a good eye for imitating nature, we can create tiny environments that soothe us, much as do the landscapes they suggest. As all of us spend more and more time sitting motionless in front of computer monitors, we have more and more need of the gentle conversation these companions provide.

Principles of feng shui, the Chinese art of placement, hold that moving water attracts chi, or life force. For that reason, fountains are placed in indoor spaces, especially inside entryways, by those seeking to attract positive energy to their homes and offices. Set your tabletop fountain on a small table, pedestal, tiled floor, or decorative base just inside your front door, in a windowside alcove, among your houseplants, or near your desk or work area. As natural humidifiers, fountains add water vapor to our air, making the surrounding environment ever more hospitable to us and to our indoor plants. Most importantly, however, the soothing, gentle sound of spilling, falling water builds a sense of quiet, peaceful, harmonious relationship to the natural world around us.

Mountain Seep

This small tabletop fountain can be created without any tools other than a sympathetic eye tuned to the opportunities that exist when moving water meets a simple assembly of natural stone. It has the shady feel of a woodland stream, where freeze and thaw expose new surfaces of bedrock to the water's caress every year. Ranging mountains contain countless springs such as this one, where clear water flows from the hillsides to fall over ledges of broken shale, tufted with mosses, ferns, and russet columbines.

The flat surfaces presented when stone first breaks from the ground allow easy stacking and stable operation. Thus, some of the best stone for this fountain can be purchased at a nearby quarry or landscape stone company. I found my stones in an Appalachian river, rounded at the edges but still flat sided and stackable.

fountain piece (constructed of loosely stacked stone)

vinyl hose

pump

reservoir

The Reservoir
• Reservoir bowl, at least 3" deep x 12" in diameter (7.5 cm deep x 30 cm in diameter)
• Clear silicone caulk (if needed to fill cracks in reservoir bowl)

The Pump
• Pump, 80 GPH (304 l per hour)
• GFCI outlet

Fountain Elements
• Flat slabs of stone: more pieces than you think you will need
• Vinyl hose: 6" (15 cm) each of $1/4$", $3/8$", $1/2$" ID (6, 9, 13 mm)

Decorative Elements
• Decorative elements, such as polished stones, tiny sculpture pieces, or small shells (optional)
• Plants, such as moss and ferns (optional)

The Mountain Seep is perfectly suited for entryways, where the soft sounds of gently running water will greet visitors as they enter.

Preparing the Reservoir

▶ Step 1: Select the Bowl

Selecting your reservoir may be as simple as digging out the brown oval ceramic baking dish that was a wedding present 20 years ago and requires only a dusting off. If no such treasure is available to you, visit flea markets and import shops to find something beautiful. It can be made of ceramic, resin, metal — anything that holds water. Seal any small leaks with clear silicone caulk.

▶ Step 2: Set up the Fountain

Set the pump in the bowl, fill the bowl, and plug in the pump. Be ready to unplug it if the water spouts into the air and out of the bowl. Adjust the flow control until you create a gentle flow a few inches high.

Decorative elements such as polished stones or seashells are wonderful additions to the rocky reservoir.

Building the Seep

▶ Step 1: Design the Layout

Stack slabs of flat stone around and finally over the pump. When you have created an island of stone and can imagine where you would like to see the stream begin, unstack the stone, cut short lengths of different sizes of hose so that they can be telescoped together to reach the place where you see the stream beginning. Fit them together, making sure that the upper end can be coaxed into a right-angled bend without crimping shut, and attach to the pump.

> **ⓑ tip** If the hose must be held in a sharp bend and the stones placed on top of it aren't enough to hold it in place, slip a piece of sturdy copper wire inside the upper end of the hose. Then bend the hose and wire together — the bent wire should hold the hose at a right angle. ▼

hose bends at 90° angle

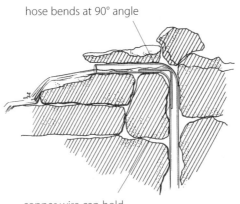

copper wire can hold hose in bent position

▶ Step 2: Put It All Together

Now rebuild your stone pile so that it contains and conceals the tubing, which ends with a right-angled bend from the vertical to the horizontal so that water comes out from beneath one of the upper stones. You may need to rebuild your waterfall several times to achieve the pattern of flow you want.

You will learn things as you move the stones around and listen to the changes in sound. Here's a way to amplify the sound in a small fountain: Create a small drop for the water with the surrounding stone overhanging slightly, forming an acoustical amphitheater.

▶ Step 3: Choose Decorative Elements and Plants

If you like, add some decorative elements, such as polished stones, tiny sculpture pieces, or small shells — whatever you feel is necessary to make the fountain uniquely suited to you and the location you intend to place it.

Add small clumps of moss and ferns, if you have access to them. If not, you can buy bromeliads (plants that thrive on nutrients derived from air and rain — not aquatic plants suitable for planting under water) and press them into recesses in the stones above water. Ferns and moss, however, can thrive with some water running over some of their roots, as long as their leaves are out of the water.

Seaside Beach

This small fountain mimics the bright light and life of the beach, where the countless details of marine life are easy to see. Here, water flows from a large seashell set upon a small stone-and-shell pile surrounding the pump. This arrangement shows off the fascinating contrast between the satiny smooth inside of most shells and their rougher, often beautifully textured outside surfaces. The only special tool you'll need is an electric drill or small handheld grinder for making a hole in the shell for the hose. If you have a collection of delicate seashells, pebbles, and beach glass, this fountain may be the ideal way to display and enjoy them. Colors that faded as the shells and stones dried in the sun will glow brightly in the clear water of a fountain.

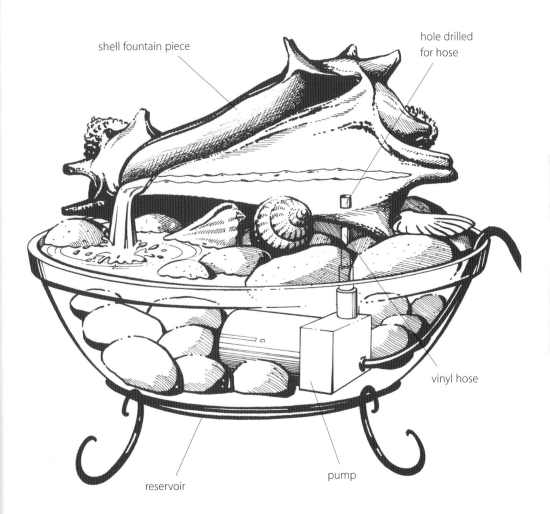

shell fountain piece

hole drilled for hose

vinyl hose

reservoir

pump

MATERIALS

The Reservoir
• Reservoir bowl, at least 3" deep x 10" in diameter (7.5 cm deep x 25 cm in diameter)

The Pump
• Pump, 80 GPH (304 l per hour)
• GFCI outlet

Fountain Elements
• Large seashell
• Vinyl hose: 12" each of ¹/₄", ³/₄" ID (6, 9 mm)

Decorative Elements
• Stones, shells, driftwood, beach glass: enough to fill the bowl

Tools
• Small handheld grinder with ¹/₄" (6 mm) or ³/₈" (9 mm) stone tip, or electric drill with bit sized for smallest hose
• Clear silicone caulk

Flowing water illuminates the iridescent interior of seashells, making them wonderful choices for the fountain piece.

Designing the Layout

▶ Step 1: Prepare the Base

First, place the pump in the bowl, leading the cord over the edge and bending it so that it drops quickly from sight. Set the flow control on the lowest setting and place a few large stones or shells around the pump. Choose flattened stones for more stable construction. Now select a large seashell, such as a conch, whelk, or abalone, to be the fountain piece. Set it in position on the stones so that it is supported above the pump. Ideally, the large opening in the shell will be oriented uppermost, so that water fills the shell and spills over its lip.

At this point, don't put much effort into the stone construction; just pile up stones stably enough to support the shell in the position you want and see if the shell and the bowl are in proportion.

▶ Step 2: Attach the Hose to the Pump

By telescoping short pieces of hose together, create a tubing assembly short enough to be hidden in the pile of stones. The largest-diameter piece of hose has to fit onto your pump's outflow, and the smallest-diameter end must fit tightly into a ⅜-inch (9 mm) hole that will be drilled in the shell. Unstack enough of the rocks so that you can fit the tubing on the pump, put water in the bowl, and plug in the pump to be sure water can pass through the assembled tubing. If the tubing seems too long, remove it and trim some of the sections with sharp scissors — without making them too short to function properly.

▶ Step 3: Position the Shell

Now place the shell on top of the piled stones. When you feel that the position of the shell is right, back up and check the overall proportion of your assembly. When you are satisfied, lift the shell and pencil a mark where the tubing will need to enter the shell.

▼ Fill the reservoir of your Seaside Beach with the most unusual shells in your collection. The flow of water will bring out their natural beauty.

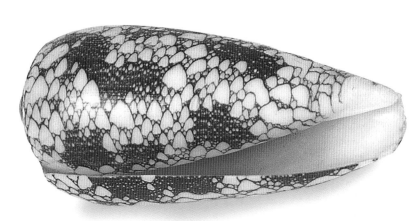

Drilling the Shell

▶ With a Handheld Grinder

A safe way to drill a hole in the shell without breaking it is with the kind of small handheld grinder that you can buy in hobby shops and hardware stores. Using a small stone grinding tip, grind through the shell and gently enlarge the hole to ⅜ inch (9 mm).

OR

▶ With an Electric Drill

If your only option is an electric drill, be very careful. Use the sharpest bit you can find, and do not press hard into the shell. Remember that the drill bit (use the all-purpose type for metal and wood) is a wedge and can split the shell if pushed into it too hard before it has a chance to cut cleanly. ▼

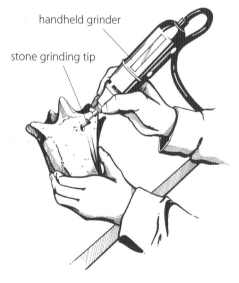

handheld grinder

stone grinding tip

⑥ tip Drilling this hole can be tricky. While drilling, check the hose's fit at frequent intervals: The tighter the fit, the better. While you're working at it, it's worth remembering the small mollusk known as a drill, which specializes in such work. This drill uses a raspy tongue to wear away the shell of a clam or scallop until a small hole is formed, then enlarges it until the animal inside can be dissolved with saliva and removed. When you find a clamshell with a perfect hole in its corner, it's the patient work of a drill.

Assembling the Fountain

▶ Step 1: Anchor the Fountain Elements

Now is the time to build your permanent assembly of stones, shells, driftwood, and beach glass to support the shell. These should be stacked loosely as much as possible. If they need to be fixed in place with clear silicone caulk, use it sparingly and only in dabs to join unruly elements to the pile. Use a hair dryer to dry any wet pieces before applying silicone caulk so that it will stick.

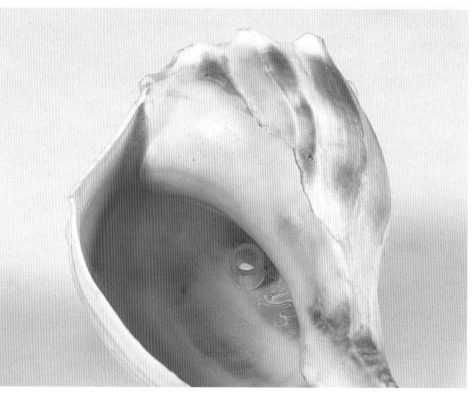

The hole should be drilled as far inside the shell as possible so that when assembled, the tubing that carries water from the pump to the shell is not seen by the casual glance.

Step 2: Test the Water Flow

Make sure the pump is set for minimum flow, then fit the tubing into the hole in the shell. Now press the larger end of your tubing assembly over the pump's outflow. Plug in the pump to see if your creation performs as planned. The shell should fill with water and overflow into the pool below. You may need to change the tilt of the shell, or change the shell itself, to make this work perfectly. Remember that you, the creator, can always fix your own mistakes.

Step 3: Decorate Your Fountain

You can add coarse beach sand or pea gravel to serve as a floor for your pool, and as a delightful texture in stone pockets. The shells of crabs, shrimp, sand dollars, and starfish can be used above the water, in positions where they stay dry. Beach glass and shells are best in wet locations where their colors show to full advantage. Even live plants such as small dune grasses can be tucked into small soil pockets in shells above the water level.

Tabletop fountains can be tucked into any small corner of your home, including bookshelves.

Lava Rock Bonsai Garden Fountain

his tabletop fountain is a good project for those with few tools other than patience. It can be used indoors or out and has no special site requirements other than sufficient light to grow the suggested plants.

This fountain is based on a design by Richard Schuck, owner of Maryland Aquatic Gardens, located in the beautiful farmlands northwest of Baltimore. He is well known for creating miniature lava rock mountains carved into intricate mazes of waterfalls and planting pockets. The result is a miniature rock garden reminiscent of the wind-burnished landscapes seen on exposed peaks and islands.

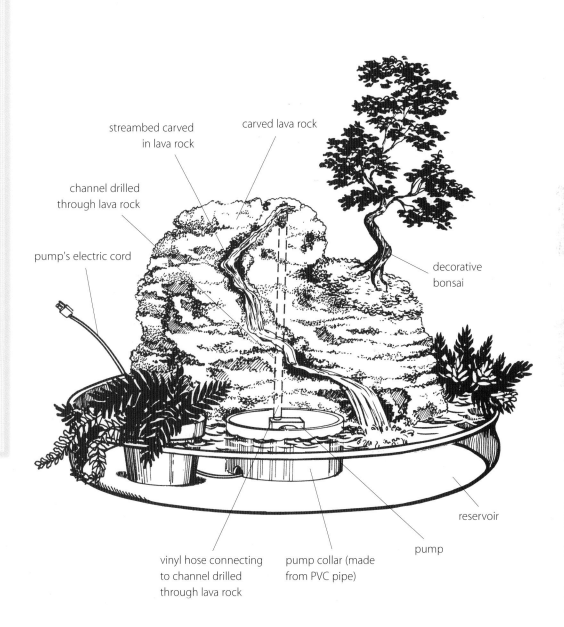

streambed carved in lava rock

carved lava rock

channel drilled through lava rock

pump's electric cord

decorative bonsai

reservoir

pump

vinyl hose connecting to channel drilled through lava rock

pump collar (made from PVC pipe)

The Reservoir
- Large bowl, at least $3^1/_2$" (8.8 cm) deep, of ceramic, metal, or resin

The Pump
- Pump, 80 GPH (304 l per hour)
- 4" (10 cm) ID PVC pipe: 4" (10 cm) section
- GFCI outlet

Fountain Elements
- Piece of lava rock, also known as featherock, sized for the bowl (available from garden centers and landscape stone companies)
- A piece of $1/_4$" (6 mm) galvanized wire mesh, also known as hardware cloth, larger than the diameter of the reservoir
- Length of $1/_2$" (13 mm) ID vinyl hose: 2–3 inches (5–8 cm) longer than the height of the lava rock

Decorative Elements
- Planting soil mix
- Mosses, ferns, small bonsai plants
- Assortment of small beach stones or large pea gravel

Tools
- Saw (for notching PVC pipe: a handsaw, bandsaw, or saber saw will work)
- Electric drill with $1/_2$" (13 mm) masonry bit
- Large plastic dishpan or mortar pan
- 2 bricks
- Tin snips
- Pocketknife

Planning the Layout

▶ Step 1: Arrange the Elements

This fountain is a good way to show off a large bowl you particularly love. Only the outside of the bowl is seen. Set the pump inside the bowl, and using 4-inch (10 cm) ID PVC pipe, fashion a pump surround, or surrounding collar. Using a saw, make a notch in the edge of this pipe for the pump cord, and if necessary trim its plastic edge down to a height at which the rock is not too high. Water will flow beneath the edge to surround the pump. Then set the lava rock on the pump surround and begin designing your garden. ▼

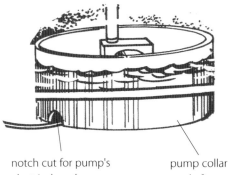

notch cut for pump's
electrical cord

pump collar
made from
PVC pipe

▶ Step 2: Design the Waterfall

The first element you need for the garden is a waterfall; you'll arrange the rest of it around this. Look at the rock, turning it in the bowl, and decide which is the top of your mountain garden. Then identify the spot from which the water will emerge. This should be high on the rock face so that you have maximum opportunity for designing a waterfall. Drawing lightly with a pencil on the rock, design the layout of the waterfall so that it changes direction as much as possible, dropping from level to level the way natural waterfalls do. If there's room for a small cascade, try to plan for the surrounding rock to "cup" the area — it will create a small pool and amplify the sound of falling water.

Cutting the Rock

▶ Step 1: Drill the Water Channel

Fit the electric drill with a ½-inch (13 mm) masonry bit and drill a channel through the rock from the spot where you've decided the water will emerge down to the underside or base of the rock. Drill from the top down; if the hole fails to reach the underside of the rock, drill up to meet it. If this takes several attempts, your mistakes will be hidden beneath the rock.

▶ Step 2: Arrange Your Work Area

For carving out your streambed, you'll need to design a special work area where you can attach the rock to the pump while testing the flow repeatedly as you carve. Plan on splashing water and bits of lava rock all over the floor and work surface. You'll need to support the rock above the pump on something more solid than the narrow PVC pump surround as you hammer and chip away rock. A good arrangement is to fill a large plastic dishpan or mortar pan with enough water to cover the pump and set it near an outlet on a workbench or kitchen counter. Arrange a couple of bricks in the bottom with the pump between them, and construct a piece of hose that fits onto the pump's outflow and into the hole in the rock. Set the rock on the bricks with the hose set into the channel you have drilled, and plug in the pump. Adjust the flow control and watch the water flow down the rock face. ▼

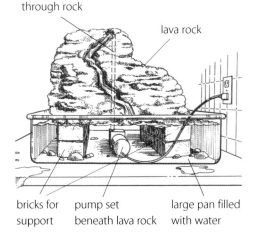

channel drilled
through rock

lava rock

bricks for
support

pump set
beneath lava rock

large pan filled
with water

▶ Step 3: Carve the Streambed

Chipping away with a pocketknife, remove material from the rock to lead the water in something like the path that you planned. Of course, your plan will need to be flexible — water has a way of flowing in unpredictable manners. Then chip out small pockets where you will later want to root ferns, moss, and small trees.

When you have finished carving out the waterfall, your piece of lava rock will sit on its bricks with water spilling from its edge into the dishpan. Fine-tune the stream with the water running, chipping away small bits here and there.

Setting Up the Fountain

▶ Step 1: Test the Water Flow

The whole thing can now be transferred to the bowl you intend to use. Set the PVC pump surround over the pump. Trim the wire mesh so that it will fit snugly inside the reservoir on top of the pump surround. Cut a hole in the screen above the pump outflow and attach the hose to the pump. Slide the channel in the carved lava rock over the other end of the hose, and gently set the rock on the screen and PVC pipe. Spread a bed of small beach stones or large gravel around the lava rock. Plug in the pump to test the water flow, and adjust as necessary.

▶ Step 2: Fine-Tune the Environment

Plug in the pump and observe the tiny ecosystem you have created. As the plants grow, they will respond to training with bonsai methods. With care, you can make them look as if they grew on the rock. If you find that you have chosen some that don't thrive in the particular light level you can provide, don't be afraid to change them for others. Your bonsai garden is a miniature world in which you can expect to learn a great deal. As in the world outside your window, your tiny garden will change every day as it teaches its subtle lessons.

Carefully tend your plants to achieve the twisted miniature forms of classic bonsai.

▶ There are innumerable variations to the Lava Rock Bonsai Fountain.

Overflowing Pottery Jar in Old Copper Basin

his small tabletop fountain is relatively easy to construct and doesn't require any special tools. It's mostly a matter of finding the parts. I used a copper basin and rustic earthenware pot that could be found in an import shop. If you have broken shards from ancient pottery, beautiful polished stones, or waterworn driftwood, this may be the place to display them. Since a drill bit is apt to heat up, use a small handheld grinder, available in most hardware stores, to make the hole for the hose in the pottery jar so that it won't crack.

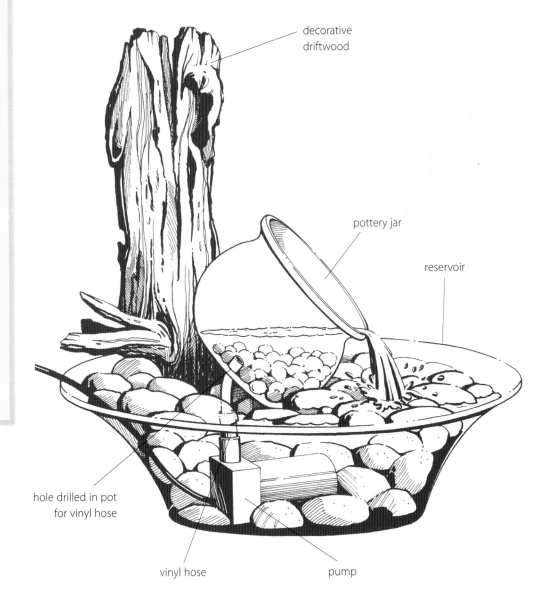

decorative driftwood

pottery jar

reservoir

hole drilled in pot for vinyl hose

vinyl hose

pump

The Reservoir
- Copper bowl, at least 3 $^1/_2$" deep x 16" in diameter (8.8 cm deep x 40 cm in diameter)
- Patina solution (for homemade recipe, see Antiquing Copper on page 114)

The Pump
- Pump, 80 GPH (304 l per hour)
- GFCI outlet

Fountain Elements
- 5–10 pounds (2.3–4.5 kg) assorted flat river stones and beach pebbles
- Earthenware pot, approximately 5" high x 3–6" in diameter (12.5 cm high x 7.5–15 cm in diameter)
- Vinyl hose to fit pump; 1" each of successive diameters

Decorative Elements
- Driftwood, arrowheads, polished stones, and other decorative elements

Tools
- Small handheld grinder with $^1/_4$" (6 mm) bit

Tall, vertical items such as this piece of driftwood will complement the mostly horizontal pottery jar. You can mount them on flat pieces of slate or plywood to help them stand steady in the basin.

Preparing the Layout

▶ Step 1: Arrange the Pump and Pot

Place the pump in the copper basin and stack some of the river stones around it for support. Arrange the pot on top of the pump and stones, leaning over at an angle. Judge the proportions of the arrangement and estimate whether there is enough distance between the lip of the pot and the outer edge of the copper basin to contain any splashing that might occur as water falls from the lip of the urn onto the stones beneath. This distance should be at least 4 inches (10 cm). Only testing with water will prove if this is sufficient. Note by eye a good point for the hose from the pump to enter the pot (centered in the bottom or slightly up the side). Pick up the pot and mark this point with a pencil.

> **tip** Some pots sold for use as planters have preexisting drainage holes. If you find one that you'd like to use as a fountain piece, don't worry if the vinyl hose is a loose fit in the drainage hole — backflow through this hole will simply decrease the amount of water spilling from the lip. If necessary, you can use silicone caulk to fill the extra space around the hose.

▶ Step 2: Drill the Pot

Set the pot upside down on a workbench. With the grinder and a grindstone bit approximately ¼ inch (6 mm) in diameter, begin grinding a hole in the pot. Keep the pot cool by dipping it in water as you drill. Unplug the grinder and rinse the grindstone under the faucet periodically to remove the paste of ground pottery that accumulates. Once the hole is drilled through the wall, enlarge it to ⅜ inch (9 mm) so that it will accept a piece of ¼-inch (6 mm) ID hose about 1 inch (2.5 cm) long. Telescope this into incrementally smaller pieces of hose until the tubing fits onto the pump's outflow fitting. ▼

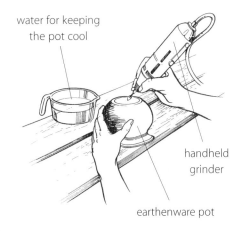

water for keeping the pot cool

handheld grinder

earthenware pot

▶ Step 3: Test the Fountain

Adjust the pump's flow control to medium and fill the copper basin with water. Place gravel, pebbles, and small stones inside the pot, enough to cover the end of the hose that protrudes from its base. Add more stones if necessary to support the pot, then plug in the pump. Once the pot is filled to overflowing and begins to spill, study the water as it pours from the lip. If you detect too much splashing, you must lower the lip by changing the angle of the pot to one more horizontal. If you want a louder sound of water, try raising the lip to increase the distance the water falls. Once you have discovered the correct relationship of the parts to each other, you can take the fountain apart and concentrate on the finishing touches. ▼

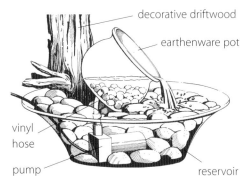

decorative driftwood

earthenware pot

vinyl hose

pump

reservoir

Be Patient!

It's very important to grind the pottery slowly and patiently. If the clay is high fired, hard, and glassy, the process will be longer and more difficult than with soft and porous earthenware. If by some chance you should break the pot while grinding the hole, don't despair — you can glue it together using two-part epoxy resin glue.

Making the Finishing Touches

▶ Step 1: Finish the Copper

Copper oxidizes in nature to a blue-green patina. If you're working with a bright copper bowl and want it to look antique, you can "encourage" it to look weathered by the following procedure.

Using a soapy kitchen scouring pad, thoroughly burnish the surface to remove any grease or protective lacquer coating. This may require considerable scrubbing. Then apply a coating of patina solution with a spray bottle or sponge (wearing rubber gloves). Use this solution in a well-ventilated location, preferably outdoors, and wear eye protection. Allow the solution to dry before assessing its effectiveness. If there has been little or no change, more scouring may be required. Two to three coats of patina solution should turn the copper a deep turquoise color, and this oxidationing should continue to develop over time. ▼

soapy scouring pad   copper basin

▶ Step 2: Finish the Ceramic Surface

The pot can be made to look old, too, especially if the clay is the low-fired soft type usually found in import shops. If possible, buy one with little or no glaze on it. If it is unglazed, rub it with a combination of wood stains, shoe polish, and latex paints to achieve the mottled, dirt-stained look of a pot long buried. If it is glazed, examine the glaze under strong light. Look for a network of fine cracks in the finish. This is known as crazing, and you can exploit it by soaking the pot in strong coffee or tea. This will stain the clay in the cracks and exaggerate the crazed pattern.

▶ Step 3: Finalize the Assembly

Replace the pot, tubing assembly, pump, and stones into the copper basin. Add more stones until the cord is covered as it runs over the lip of the basin, fill with water, and plug the pump into a GFCI outlet. This is the time to add favorite rocks, fossils, arrowheads, driftwood, and small bones to your desert fountain to enhance the sense of long-ago cultures.

▶ Setting your fountain in front of a window, whether in a kitchen alcove or on a pedestal, will reinforce the connection to nature that it creates.

An old earthen jar and antiqued copper basin are perfect fountain elements to accentuate a rustic setting.

Small Tabletop *Tsukubai*

*T*his small tabletop fountain is relatively easy to make and requires far fewer special materials and techniques than most. Armed only with a sharp handsaw and pocketknife for working with bamboo, you can practice your design sense in a forgiving medium that produces a working fountain in a couple of hours.

This fountain makes a beautiful vase. In it you can offer a changing display of living flowers and vegetation. A flower can float in the water or be held by the bamboo strips. Especially satisfying displays for each season include adding a fresh sprig of bamboo or small branch of new oak leaves in spring, Japanese anemones in summer, scarlet Japanese maple leaves in autumn, and a twig of wind-twisted pine in winter. A single short candle set on the supports can lend exactly the right note of warmth after dark.

decorative plant

chair cane

vinyl hose

bamboo spout

bamboo support pieces

pump

ceramic bowl

The Reservoir

• Ceramic bowl at least 3¹/₂" deep x 12" in diameter (8.8 cm deep x 30 cm in diameter)

The Pump

• Pump, 80 GPH (304 l per hour) with variable flow control
• GFCI outlet

Fountain Elements

• ¹/₂–³/₄" (13–19 mm) diameter bamboo: 2 pieces, approximately 1' (30 cm) each
• 1¹/₂" (3.8 cm) diameter bamboo approximately 1' (30 cm)
• ¹/₄" (6 mm) ID vinyl hose: 1' (30 cm), plus short lengths of larger sizes, as needed
• Chair cane, natural twine, or 18-gauge copper wire
• 10–14-gauge copper wire: 3" (7.5 cm), for bending hose

Tools

• Sharp saw
• Vise or clamps
• Sandpaper
• Pocketknife

Constructing the Bamboo Fountain Piece

▶ Step 1: Cut the Support Pieces

Cut two pieces of ½-inch (13 mm) diameter bamboo to lengths long enough to overhang your ceramic bowl by an inch (2.5 cm) or so on each side (see Working with Bamboo on page 41 for tips and techniques). They should be cut so that they have nodes at each end, providing a finished, thickened termination. Set this pair of sticks across the top of the bowl, covering no more than one-third of it; they'll serve to support the bamboo spout.

▶ Step 2: Cut the Spout

The spout will be roughly 6 inches (15 cm) long. Select a piece of bamboo about 1½ inches (3.8 cm) in diameter and a foot (30 cm) in length. If there is a wall in the bamboo, cut the bamboo with a sharp saw at a right angle about an inch (2.5 cm) beyond it, so that the wall is included in the spout — this will be the back end. Approximately 6 inches (15 cm) from this spot, cut the front end of the spout at a sharp angle, at least 45 degrees. ▼

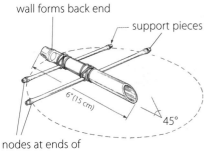

wall forms back end

support pieces

6"(15 cm)

45°

nodes at ends of support pieces

▶ Step 3: Drill a Hole for the Hose

The hose should enter the spout about two-thirds of the way from the front, on the bottom. Mark this spot and cut away the bamboo wall by making two parallel saw cuts, then carving out the bamboo between them with a pocketknife. Alternatively, you can drill a hole with a ⅝-inch (16 mm) Forstner bit. Make this hole only as large as necessary to accommodate your ¼-inch (6 mm) ID hose.

Cut a length of this hose about 6 inches (15 cm) long and push it into the hole and toward the front of the spout, stopping before it becomes easily visible from the front. ▼

ⓑ tip In order to make the tubing bend tightly enough to keep the pump beneath the bamboo, slide a piece of heavy copper wire into the tubing, trim it to length, and bend the tubing and wire to the desired shape.

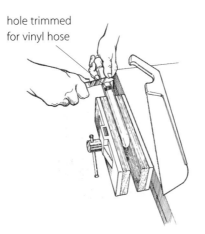

hole trimmed for vinyl hose

▶ Step 4: Attach the Spout to the Support Pieces

Using twine, 18-gauge copper wire, or chair cane soaked in hot water to make it flexible, lash the two bamboo supporting pieces together so that the spout crosses them. The spout should be positioned so that it will discharge water into the center of the bowl. Use a figure-eight pattern to make neat wraps, placing each one beside the last rather than allowing them to overlap and bunch. Tuck the end underneath the last few wraps, pull it tight, and cut the end off close. The hose should fit between the crossbars of the platform to hang down into the bowl. ▼

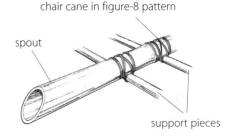

chair cane in figure-8 pattern

spout

support pieces

Setting Up Your Fountain

Now adjust the pump's flow control to its lowest setting, place the pump in the bowl, set the platform and spout over it, and connect the hose to the spout, telescoping pieces as necessary.

Fill the bowl with water and plug in the pump. The water should flow gently from the spout, without splashing.

3 Projects in Bamboo and Wood

The warmth of wood can prove irresistible. Its soft coloration and often dramatic grain patterns make it a natural choice for anyone designing a piece of water art. It is soft enough to be formed by the tools in many home workshops, and so abundantly available that it is usually not terribly expensive.

Another advantage that wood construction has over concrete casting is that it can be modified as you go along, as compared to the go-for-broke sensation of pouring concrete into a mold and waiting for the moment of truth. As you fit wooden parts together, you may decide to change the design of your fountain base. It's not hard to see in advance what the consequences of the change will be.

When it comes into contact with water, however, wood does not usually last as long as metal or stone. It is difficult to get it to hold water without any leaks. For this reason, I use it only where leaks won't matter — a half whiskey barrel used outdoors, for instance. For added protection you can give the wood a waterproof lining. For indoor use you can protect the wood with finish and keep water from splashing onto it. Some woods, such as redwood, cedar, and cypress, are naturally rot resistant and can be used indoors or out without a special finish.

Working with Bamboo

Bamboo, a member of the grass family, is used in water gardens and fountains throughout the world. This beautiful natural material is found growing wild in most neighborhoods where the temperature rarely falls below freezing. If yours is not one of these, you can order bamboo from one of the sources listed in appendix C.

Cutting and Sawing

Cutting bamboo for support and spout pieces is much easier if you can hold the bamboo in a vise or clamp it to a sturdy countertop while sawing. To cut bamboo, use the finest and the sharpest saw you can lay your hands on. If you have access to a bandsaw, use it. Bamboo's surface contains fibers that, when cut with a dull saw, tear loose and require considerable peeling to neaten.

Be aware also of the location of the natural walls in the bamboo. These occur at the joints, or nodes, and give the material its distinctive appearance.

You will have to drill out any wall that occurs where a hose must pass inside the bamboo. This makes construction with bamboo complicated; rather than avoid these beautiful features, see to it that they are located where drilling will be easy or unnecessary.

Wrapping with Twine or Wire

Because it is a grass, bamboo is almost certain to split. In use, the outside usually dries, while the inside is kept wet. This causes swelling inside and shrinking outside, building up pressure that is relieved by the formation of a crack. The best approach to this is to expect it and use it as an opportunity for further decoration. As soon as you have cut your pieces, wrap them at several points — especially near the slanted end of the horizontal arm — with a natural twine or copper wire. Wrap the wire around two or three times with only one overlap at the end, located at the back or bottom so as to be unobtrusive. These wraps, in combination with the mossy look of old bamboo spouts as they soften and age, are an important element of the Zen tradition in garden design.

Bamboo grows wild in most regions. Check with the landowner before harvesting.

When it's cut apart, you can see the interior walls that lend bamboo its unique character.

Bamboo Dipper

This dipper can be made in any size for any fountain. It is particularly suitable for the Small Tabletop *Tsukubai*, the Cedar Water Garden with Bamboo Flute, the Birdshower Fountain, the Portable *Tsukubai* Fountain, and the Concrete Coin Basin with Bamboo Spout, all of which are adaptations of the Japanese *Tsukubai*, a fountain often found outside ceremonial teahouses. Before entering the teahouse, celebrants pause in front of the *Tsukubai*, a stone basin filled with clean water by a bamboo spout. Here they bend low to dip water with a bamboo ladle and wash their hands.

Review Working with Bamboo on page 41, which describes the tools required for cutting bamboo. You must have a very sharp handsaw to avoid tearing the surface fibers. The fine blade of a hacksaw also works well.

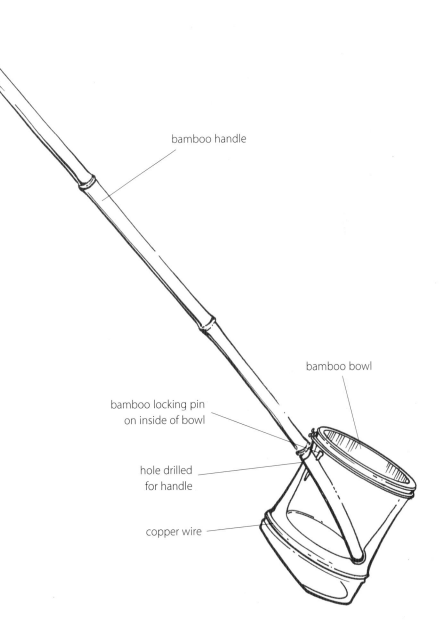

bamboo handle

bamboo bowl

bamboo locking pin on inside of bowl

hole drilled for handle

copper wire

ATERIALS

Dipper Elements

- Short length of bamboo that's about 2" (5 cm) in diameter, with one wall (for bowl)
- 2' (60 cm) of bamboo that's about $1/4$" (6 mm) in diameter (for handle)
- Tiny branches of bamboo (for pegs)
- Copper wire for wrapping, about 18 gauge (twine or rattan also works)

Tools

- Sharp saw (bandsaw if available)
- Sheet of coarse sandpaper, about 80 grit (can use belt sander if available)
- Vise (if available)
- Electric drill with drill bit sized for handle (about $1/4$", or 6 mm)
- Drill bit sized for peg (about $1/8$", or 3 mm)
- Wire nippers

Participants in the Japanese tea ceremony, which usually takes place in a teahouse like the one featured here, often use a bamboo dipper to ladle water from a nearby source, such as a *tsukubai* fountain, to cleanse their hands and faces before entering.

▶ Step 1: Cut and Sand the Bowl

From a section of the 2-inch (5 cm) diameter bamboo, cut a bowl about 2 inches high. To take advantage of the beautiful concave bottom this gives your dipper, make the bottom cut ¼ inch (6 mm) below one of the nodes in the bamboo. Then, using a saw and sandpaper, bevel a flat spot in the bottom edge so that the bowl will rest at an angle. Sand all edges. ▼

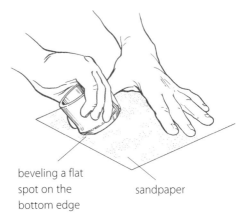

beveling a flat
spot on the
bottom edge   sandpaper

▶ Step 2: Cut the Handle

Cut a handle from ¼-inch (6 mm) bamboo about 14 inches (35 cm) long, with a joint at one end and another about 2½ inches (6.3 cm) from the other end. The end that is 2½ inches (6.3 cm) from a node will be inserted through a hole in the side of the bowl.

▶ Step 3: Drill the Bowl

Placing the bowl in a vise or holding it securely, drill a hole the size of the unjointed end of the handle through one side of the bowl, at a tilted angle and near the top. Make this hole a very tight fit — start with a bit that's a size smaller than you think you'll need. You can enlarge the hole with a larger bit or a whittling knife if necessary. Once the bit has passed through the side and into the interior of the bowl, allow it to penetrate slightly into the opposite side down near the bottom of the bowl. This makes a socket for the end of the handle; it should not pass through the side of the bowl.

▶ Step 4: Insert the Handle

Enlarge the hole if necessary until you can gently tap the handle into place. The joint in the handle near the bowl should end up tight against the outside of the bowl. The remaining 2½ inches (6.3 cm) of handle should reach across the bowl and project into the socket in the other side. Trim the length as necessary.

On the handle just inside the bowl, mark the location where the locking pin should be inserted to keep the handle from slipping out of its hole. Drill a hole about ⅛ inch (3 mm) through it, and cut a pin from tiny bamboo branch material to drive into this hole. This pin locks the handle into the bowl.

▶ Step 5: Wrap the Bowl

Undo the assembly in order to wrap the bowl of the dipper with 18-gauge wire. The wire will help control cracking. Making the wraps neat, twist the ends together and nip them off with two twists projecting. Fold this stub over and file it smooth to the touch. Then tap the handle back into place and insert the locking pin. ▼

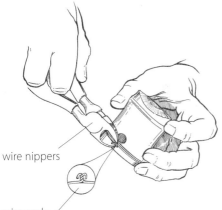

wire nippers

wire ends
twisted together

Cedar Water Garden with Bamboo Flute

This small water garden and fountain can be used indoors or out. The western red cedar frame is weather resistant, so you can enjoy a pond on your deck or patio. A sunny location is best; this will allow various flowering water plants and even a few fish to flourish in the 10-gallon (38 l) reservoir. You will need basic woodworking tools for the construction.

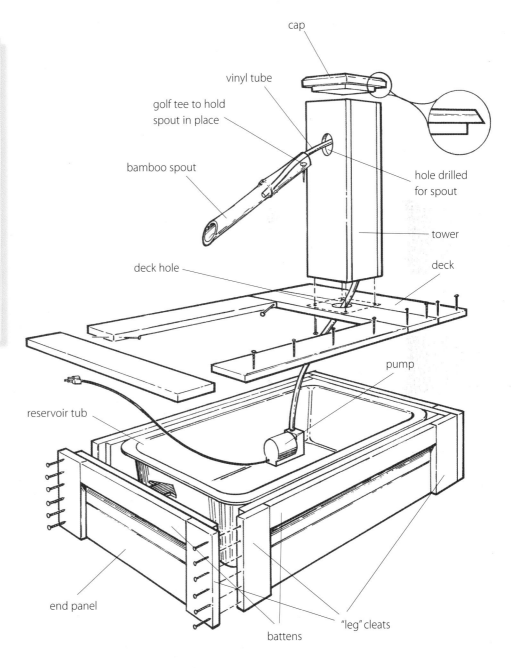

cap

vinyl tube

golf tee to hold
spout in place

bamboo spout

hole drilled
for spout

tower

deck hole

deck

pump

reservoir tub

end panel

battens

"leg" cleats

$\mathscr{M}$ ATERIALS

The Reservoir

- Rectangular plastic tub, approximately 24 x 30 x 6" (60 x 75 x 15 cm), or plywood box with rubber pond liner

The Pump

- Pump with grounded cord, 80–140 GPH (304–532 l per hour)
- GFCI outlet

Fountain Elements

- $^3/_4$ x 5 $^1/_2$" (1.9 x 14 cm) western red cedar fencing board: about 40' (12 m)
- 1–2" (2.5–5 cm) diameter bamboo: a few feet (about 1 m)
- Golf tee
- Vinyl hose: 3' (1 m) ID to fit pump's outflow

Tools

- Table saw
- 4d penny galvanized finish nails and hammer
- Sharp handsaw
- Sandpaper, 80 to 100 grit
- Handheld drill or drill press with hole saw same diameter as bamboo
- 4 drywall screws, 1$^1/_2$–2" (3.8–5 cm) long
- Phillips-head screwdriver

The ideal location for growing water lilies is in deep, quiet water in strong sun — they need plenty of sun in order to flower, and they don't like to be splashed.

Building the Cedar Frame

▶ Step 1: Buy or Make the Reservoir

First select the reservoir tub for your fountain. This can be a plastic mortar pan (available in most hardware stores for mixing cement), or you can construct one yourself of plywood lined with a rubber pond liner. The best size is about 24 by 30 by 6 inches (60 by 75 by 15 cm), but you can adapt the design to any size you have room for. If you opt to build your own and line it, fold the liner loosely into the box and staple it every inch (2.5 cm) or so to the outside top edge. ▼

rubber pond liner

plywood reservoir

▶ Step 2: Construct the Frame

Construct a frame of western red cedar to surround this reservoir. You'll need:
- 2 side panels
- 2 end panels
- 2 side battens
- 2 end battens
- 4 "leg" cleats for the sides
- 4 "leg" cleats for the ends

Since the frame's sides should be approximately the same height as the sides of the tub, you will probably need a table saw to rip the 5½-inch (14 cm) fencing to width and assemble side and end panels of the necessary height. These are held together by cedar end cleats and reinforced by adding narrow (1½ inches, or 3.8 cm, wide) cedar battens to the top edges. Overlap the end cleats to form "legs," as shown on page 47.

▶ Step 3: Add the Deck

Next, you'll add a cedar deck that's 3½ inches (8.8 cm) wide — enough to conceal the edge of the reservoir. On the short side that will eventually be the back of the fountain, double this dimension to yield a deck platform wide enough to accommodate the tower and spout, and to conceal the pump below. Attach these pieces to the frame panels with galvanized 4d penny finish nails. (See the illustration on page 47 for reference.)

Building the Tower

▶ Step 1: Make the Bamboo Spout

Select a piece of bamboo 1¾ to 2 inches (4.4 to 5 cm) in diameter and about 18 inches (45 cm) long, preferably with a node or wall occurring about 6 inches (15 cm) from one end. Make this the pointed end and cut the bamboo at a sharp 30-degree angle. The other end, which will fit into a hole in the tower, is cut square. Drill a ³⁄₁₆-inch (5 mm) hole through the outside shell of the bamboo about an inch (2.5 cm) from this end on the bottom side. This will be for a golf tee, which holds the spout in the hole. Drill out the wall in the bamboo and sand all end cuts. ▼

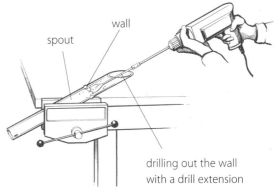

wall

spout

drilling out the wall with a drill extension

▶ Step 2: Assemble the Side Panels

Cut two lengths of red cedar, each measuring 5 by 18 inches (12.5 by 45 cm), for the front and back of the tower. Choose one length for the front panel — you must now drill a hole that is the same size as the bamboo spout into this panel, at an angle. This is best done with a Forstner bit or a hole saw in a drill press, although if you're strong and steady, a handheld drill may be sufficient. Set the piece on the drill press platform, resting it on enough scrap to allow the saw and pilot bit to cut all the way through it. Adjust the piece so that the saw enters the wood centered at a point about one-third of the way from the top, at a 20-degree angle so that the spout will slope downward from the tower. Clamp the wood and bring the saw slowly into it to produce a clean hole.

Cut two lengths of red cedar, each measuring 3½ inches by 18 inches (8.8 cm by 45 cm), for the tower sides. Then go ahead and nail together the tower pieces with galvanized 4d penny finish nails. ▼

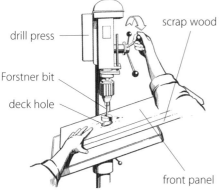

drill press

scrap wood

Forstner bit

deck hole

front panel

▶ Step 3: Assemble the Cap

Then you'll make a cap for the tower by cutting a 5½-inch (14 cm) cedar square and beveling its top edge on the table saw. Nail a cedar block 3¼ by 3¼ inches (8.1 by 8.1 cm) to the bottom as a flange to keep the cap in place. ▼

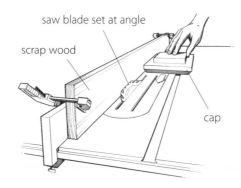

saw blade set at angle

scrap wood

cap

> **⑥ tip** When beveling on a table saw, clamp a scrap of wood to the fence so that the saw blade, set at a 45-degree angle, can cut into the scrap. This arrangement produces a more consistent bevel than when the stock is fed between the blade and the fence. It's also safer.

▶ Step 4: Drill the Deck Hole for the Vinyl Hose

Because it's being oriented square to the piece of wood it's drilled in, this hole is far easier to drill. Using the same hole saw, cut the hole in the wide back deck, centered 3 inches (7.5 cm) from the water side.

▶ Step 5: Attach the Tower to the Deck

To attach the tower to the deck, set the tower in place centered left to right and about ½ inch (13 mm) back from the water side. Scratch lines in the deck to mark its outside edges, remove the tower, and drill small pilot holes, two per side. Then use sharp drywall screws (each 1½ to 2 inches, or 3.8 to 5 cm, long) from underneath the deck to attach the tower to the deck. ▼

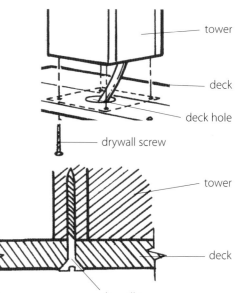

tower

deck

deck hole

drywall screw

tower

deck

drywall screw

Setting Up Your Water Garden

▶ Step 1: Attach the Hose and Test the Water Flow

Place the pump in the reservoir tub and run the cord over the edge toward the back. Set the cedar frame with its tower attached over the tub. Making sure your vinyl hose will fit your pump's outflow (if it doesn't, use the telescoping technique described on page 7 to ensure a good fit), feed the hose into the tower so that it can be led through the deck hole and attached to the pump. The other end should be led through the slanting spout hole in the tower. Now slide the spout over the hose and, reaching into the tower, fit the golf tee into the retaining hole to keep the spout from dropping out of the tower. Adjust the hose so that it doesn't show inside the bamboo, and place the cap on the tower.

Fill the tub with water and plug in the pump. Adjust the flow of water so that it doesn't splash, and relax to the comforting sound it creates.

During the colder months of winter, tropical aquatic plants will often thrive quite happily if brought indoors and replanted in a water-filled, plastic-lined windowbox set in a sunny window.

▶ Step 2: Add Decorative Elements

This fountain is large enough to create a small, portable pond. It's an excellent location for marginal bog plants, which stand proudly in submerged pots, their roots spreading across the floor of the tub. Floating species such as water hyacinths will bloom if there's sufficient sunlight, and a few small goldfish will be able to live in the roomy pool beneath them. If you place this fountain outdoors, frogs, toads, and dragonflies will be naturally drawn to its waters. Indoors, it can offer a winter haven for your tropical pond plants.

Cedar and Bamboo Fountain for a Pond

This fountain, a variation of the Cedar Water Garden with Bamboo Flute on page 47, creates a tower and spout for use with an existing pond or pool. You can install it beside a half barrel or stone trough if you don't have a pond. It creates the illusion of a rustic pipe supplied by water mysteriously flowing from some natural source.

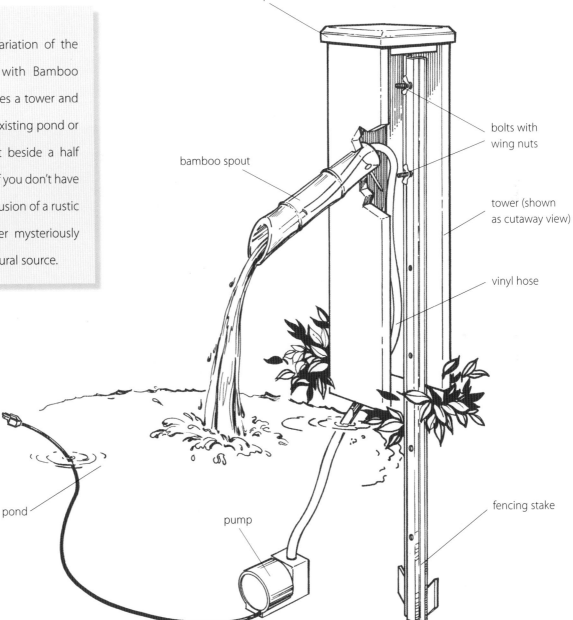

cap

bolts with wing nuts

bamboo spout

tower (shown as cutaway view)

vinyl hose

pond

pump

fencing stake

MATERIALS

The Reservoir
- Existing pond, pool, or other large tub of water

The Pump
- Pump, at least 140 GPH (532 l per hour; the pond's pre-existing filter pump will probably work)
- GFCI outlet

Fountain Elements
- $1^1/_2$–2" (3.8–5 cm) diameter bamboo: a few feet (about 1 m)
- Golf tee
- $3/_4$ x $5^1/_2$" (1.9 x 14 cm) cedar fencing, about 12' (3.7 m)
- Fencing stake of folded metal with holes for attachment
- Vinyl hose; enough to reach spout from pump, same diameter as pump's outflow

Tools
- Table saw
- Sandpaper: 100 grit
- Handheld drill or drill press with hole saw of the same diameter as bamboo
- 4d penny galvanized finish nails
- Hammer
- $1/_4$" (6 mm) drill bit for (bolts)
- Stainless-steel round-head bolts ($3/_{16}$", or 5 mm, in diameter; 2", or 5 cm, long) and wing nuts

Making the Bamboo Spout

▶ Step 1: Cut the Spout

Select a piece of bamboo 1½ to 2 inches (4.4 to 5 cm) in diameter and about 18 inches (45 cm) long, preferably with a wall occurring about 6 inches (15 cm) from one end. Make this the pointed end, and cut the bamboo at a sharp 30-degree angle. The other end, which will fit into the hole in the tower, is cut square. (See Working with Bamboo on page 41 for more information.) Use a spade bit to drill out the wall. If you need to elongate the shaft in order to reach the wall, use a drill extension (available at building supply stores). ▼

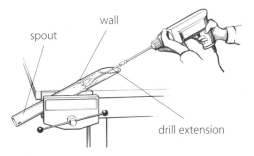

spout
wall
drill extension

▶ Step 2: Drill Hole for Golf Tee Support

Drill a ³⁄₁₆-inch (5 mm) hole through the bamboo shell about an inch (2.5 cm) from the square end on the bottom side. This hole will allow a golf tee to hold the spout in the hole. Drill out the wall in the bamboo and sand all end cuts.

◀ If you live in colder regions and stock your pond with small fish, check with local sources to determine how deep the pond needs to be to allow the fish to overwinter safely.

Constructing the Tower

▶ Step 1: Cut the Tower Parts

The tower is a slender box of cedar, 5 inches (12.5 cm) square and approximately 30 inches (75 cm) high — you should adjust the height dimension to the site and size of your pond. Cut the parts from the cedar fencing on a table saw.

- 2 panels for the front and back, approximately 5 inches (12.5 cm) wide and 30 inches (75 cm) long
- 2 side panels, approximately 3½ inches (8.8 cm) wide and 30 inches (75 cm) long
- 1 cap piece, approximately 5½ inches (14 cm) square
- 1 flange block, approximately 3¼ inches (8.1 cm) square

Bevel the top edge of the cap on the table saw, then nail the flange block to the bottom of the cap to keep the cap in place. ▼

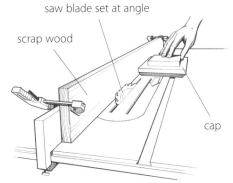

saw blade set at angle
scrap wood
cap

▶ Step 2: Drill the Spout Hole

Decide which panel will be the front panel of the tower. A large hole, the same size of the bamboo spout, must be drilled into this panel, at an angle. This is best done by clamping the panel in a drill press and using a Forstner bit or hole saw. If you're strong and steady, a handheld drill may be sufficient. It's easiest to do this before you assemble the tower, while you can work on the front piece alone. Set the piece on the drill press platform, adjusting the platform so that the saw enters the wood centered at a point about one-third of the way from the top, at a 20-degree angle so that the spout will slope downward from the tower. Rest the part to be drilled on enough scrap to allow the saw and pilot bit to cut all the way through it at an angle. Clamp the wood and bring the saw slowly into it to produce a clean hole. ▼

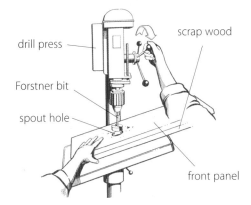

drill press
Forstner bit
spout hole
scrap wood
front panel

Setting Up Your Fountain

▶ **Step 3: Assemble the Tower**

Fasten together the tower panels with 4d penny galvanized finish nails.

▶ **Step 4: Drill the Tower for Attachment to the Stake**

Lay the tower and metal stake on a bench with the stake outside the tower, centered up the back side, so that it reaches 1 inch (2.5 cm) from the top of the tower. Mark the locations of two holes near the top of the stake. Then drill through the tower at these points so that when the tower is dropped over the stake after it is driven into the ground at the side of the pond, you can use bolts and wing nuts to fasten the tower to the stake. ▼

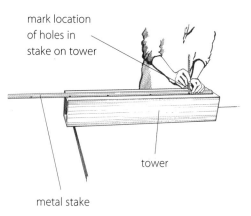

mark location of holes in stake on tower

tower

metal stake

▶ **Step 1: Assemble the Fountain**

Drive the stake into the ground next to the pond, being careful to stop when the top holes in the stake have reached the correct height for the tower. Drop the tower over the stake and insert bolts into the holes as well as through those in the stake. Putting the wing nuts on the inside of the tower, tighten them on the bolts.

Now feed a length of hose down the tower into the pond. Push the other end out of the spout hole. Slipping the spout over this projecting hose and into the spout hole, push the golf tee into its hole to hold the spout in the tower. Adjust the hose so that it does not show in the bamboo and attach it to a pump. Most ponds already have pumps in them for filtration; if so, attach the hose to your pump's outflow. If your pond has no pump, use a small fountain pump with a head sufficiently high to reach your spout (a pump rated for 140 GPH, or 532 l per hour, will probably be large enough). ▶

▶ **Step 2: Test the Water Flow**

Plug in the pump and adjust the flow control if necessary. This fountain should be able to run fairly forcefully if your pond is large enough so that splashing is not a problem. If, however, the water splashes out of the pool or half barrel, you will need to reduce the flow from the pump.

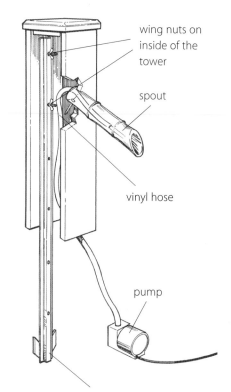

wing nuts on inside of the tower

spout

vinyl hose

pump

metal fencing stake

▶ In most regions this fountain can run all year long, so long as the pond is deep enough to allow the pump to rest below any ice that may form during the winter.

Shishi Odoshi, or Deer Scare

The *Shishi Odoshi* may have been devised by the ancient Japanese for keeping deer from their gardens. Also called the water hammer, it has been used for centuries in Zen ceremonial gardens, where the rhythmic hollow clunk of the hammer as it strikes a rock helps draw your attention into this tranquil world of stone and water.

This fountain has two parts: the faucet and the hammer. In order to assemble these pieces, you must be able to cut and drill clean angles and holes in tough bamboo walls. This is made far easier with a band saw and a drill press, although with skill you can work around it with a handheld drill and coping saw or hacksaw.

This fountain tends to splash and drip. It is important to scale it carefully for your chosen location. It will be far easier to maintain it in an outdoor location, where the occasional drip can be absorbed into the surrounding garden.

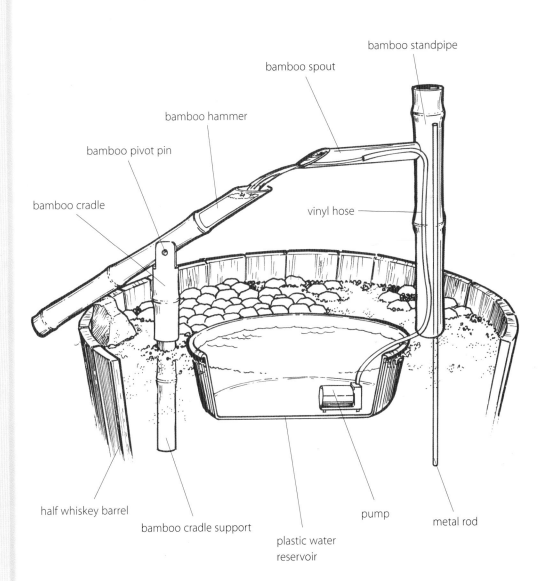

bamboo standpipe

bamboo spout

bamboo hammer

bamboo pivot pin

bamboo cradle

vinyl hose

half whiskey barrel

bamboo cradle support

pump

metal rod

plastic water reservoir

When the hammer fills with water it becomes unbalanced and falls, spilling the water into the reservoir. As the empty hammer rises, its end hits the stone behind it with an abrupt "clack."

The Reservoir
- Half whiskey barrel
- Reservoir for water: round or rectangular, black plastic or flexible liner or bucket 9 x 12 x 5" (22.5 x 30 x 12.5 cm)
- Potting soil

The Pump
- Pump with grounded cord for outdoor use, 80 GPH (304 l per hour)
- GFCI outlet nearby, or GFCI extension cord

Fountain Elements
- Vinyl hose: 3' (1 m), sized for pump you intend to use
- Metal rod, approximately 18" (45 cm) long
- **Hammer:** Bamboo piece approximately 15" (37.5 cm) long, 1 inch (2.5 cm) in diameter
- **Cradle:** Bamboo piece approximately 12" (30 cm) long, 2 inches (5 cm) in diameter
- **Pivot pin:** Bamboo piece approximately 6" (15 cm) long, $3/8$ inch (9 mm) in diameter
- **Cradle support:** Bamboo piece approximately 12" (30 cm) long that will slide snugly inside the 2" (5 cm) diameter bamboo cradle piece
- **Spout:** Bamboo piece approximately 6" (15 cm) long, $5/8$ inch (16 mm) in diameter

Tools
- Paper and pencil
- Bandsaw, coping saw, or hacksaw
- Sandpaper: 100 grit
- Drill press or variable-speed handheld drill with Forstner bits in several sizes

Planning the Layout

▶ Step 1: Sketch the Dimensions

This fountain requires fairly precise planning. The water hammer is relatively small (although there is no reason why you couldn't scale this up to several feet in height and install it at ground level) and installed into the planting area of an earth-filled half-barrel planter. You may find it helpful to sketch the parts full sized on a large sheet of paper.

The half barrel I used was 18 inches (45 cm) high by 24 inches (60 cm) in diameter. The water was held in a black plastic tub. The faucet was a *standpipe,* or vertical piece, of 1½-inch (3.8 cm) diameter bamboo rising 12 inches (30 cm) high with an inserted spout ⅝ inch (16 mm) in diameter by 4 inches (10 cm) long. The hammer was 10 inches (25 cm) long, supported in a cradle made from 2-inch (5 cm) bamboo that is 8 inches (20 cm) high. If these dimensions don't work for the setup available to you, this will become obvious when you draw the fountain layout. You can then adjust them as needed.

▶ Step 2: Make the Reservoir

Position the half barrel in the location you've planned for the fountain, and fill it with good garden soil. Form the reservoir in the center of the soil by burying a plastic bucket, tub, or flexible pond liner. There should be a margin of soil all around the reservoir so that you have room to install the faucet and hammer beside it. You can ultimately cover this with a bed of beach stones interrupted by plantings of bamboo or other ornamental grasses. ▼

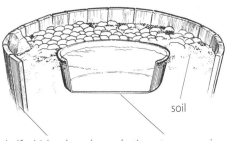

soil

half whiskey barrel   plastic water reservoir

Forming the Faucet

▶ Step 1: Cut the Standpipe

Cut a piece of bamboo about 1½ inches (3.8 cm) in diameter to a length of 12 inches (30 cm) for the standpipe. Arrange to have one of the nodes near the top to serve as a seal for the end.

▶ Step 2: Assemble the Spout

Cut a spout 4 inches (10 cm) long, with no nodes, from bamboo approximately ⅝ inch (16 mm) in diameter. (This piece can be of any diameter as long as the vinyl tubing from the hose will fit into it and it can be inserted into the standpipe — select a piece for which you have a corresponding Forstner bit or hole saw.) This spout should be cut at a sharp angle on one end and square on the other; sand its edges as necessary.

Drill a hole for the spout in the standpipe at a point about 9 inches (22.5 cm) high. Cut a length of vinyl tubing about 2 feet (60 cm) long and push it into this hole and down the standpipe. Allow about 3 inches (7.5 cm) to project from the hole. Then slide the spout piece over the hose and push it into the hole. It should be a tight fit so that it stays put. If it's loose, make a small wedge of bamboo and jam it into the hole beneath the spout to hold it tight. ▼

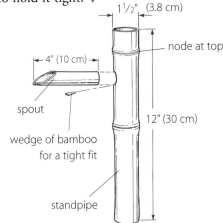

1½" (3.8 cm)

node at top

4" (10 cm)

spout

wedge of bamboo
for a tight fit

12" (30 cm)

standpipe

Step 3: Anchor the Standpipe

The standpipe of the faucet is supported by a rigid piece of metal rod. Simply push the rod into the soil until it is firmly anchored and slide the faucet with its hose onto the rod.

Step 4: Test the Water Flow

The vinyl hose must be run over the edge of the reservoir into the water, where it is attached to a pump of about 80 GPH (304 l per hour). Plug this pump into a GFCI outlet or extension cord and test the faucet. Its stream of water should land in the reservoir. Adjustments to the flow control on the pump or to the position of the faucet's support stake may be necessary.

A small pivot pin holds the hammer in place.

Forming the Hammer and Cradle

Step 1: Cut the Hammer

This step cannot be planned exactly, because you'll need to experiment with balance points before you can know how long to make the hammer. Begin by cutting a hammer piece of bamboo approximately 1 inch (2.5 cm) in diameter as follows: Clamp the bamboo piece to a bench, or grasp it securely. Make a diagonal cut near one of the walls so that the point of the tip is about 4 inches (10 cm) from the wall. This end of the hammer collects water from the faucet. When the weight of the water is sufficient, the hammer falls, spilling water and returning to an upright position with a thump against the rim of the wooden barrel. Temporarily trim the other end of the hammer so that the whole hammer piece is about 12 inches (30 cm) long. You will cut it to final length later. ▼

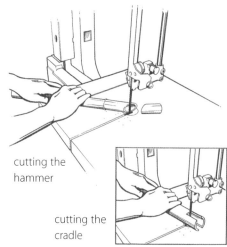

cutting the hammer

cutting the cradle

Step 2: Construct the Cradle

Cut an 8-inch (20 cm) length from bamboo that is 2 inches (5 cm) in diameter; this will form the cradle for the hammer. It may be a bit high at first; you can trim it later. With a bandsaw or coping saw, cut a wide slot 2 inches (5 cm) deep into the top of the cradle. Cut and sand the flat arms at the sides of this slot so that they are rounded.

Find a smooth piece of small bamboo about ⅜ inch (9 mm) in diameter. Cut this to form the pivot pin, about 4 inches (10 cm) long. One end should include a node; this will make it thick enough to prevent it from sliding through the hole it will rest in. Leave the other end long for later trimming.

Now drill a hole large enough to accept the pivot pin through each of the arms of the cradle, centered about ¾ inch (19 mm) from the top. Make sure the pivot pin can slide into place in the cradle, through these two holes. ▼

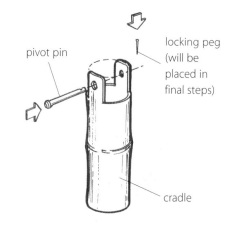

pivot pin

locking peg (will be placed in final steps)

cradle

▶ Step 3: Assemble the Hammer

Now set the hammer in the cradle, resting temporarily on top of the pivot pin so that its pointed end is up in the air. Find the balance point, then select the spot for the pivot hole somewhere between the balance point and the node that forms the bottom of the water cup. Drill a hole through the hammer at this point and slide the pivot pin through it so that the hammer can swing freely.

▶ Step 4: Install the Hammer

The hammer must be supported so that it moves without jiggling out of alignment. Select a piece of bamboo the right size to slide inside the cradle, and about 12 inches (30 cm) long, then drive it into the soil beside the reservoir, across from the faucet. Install the cradle and hammer by sliding the cradle over this bamboo stake. The long, untrimmed end of the hammer should rest on the rim of the half barrel. ▼

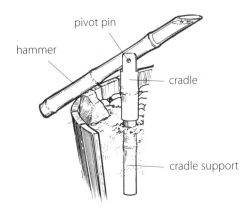

▶ Step 5: Trim the Hammer

Fill the reservoir, plug in the pump, and watch the faucet fill the hammer. Lift the back of the hammer with your finger to dump the water. From the weight you are lifting, you should get some idea how much to trim off the hammer's back end so that it will tip with no lift from you. Cut off this extra material a little at a time, setting the hammer in the cradle each time to test it. It should sit with pointed-cup end up when empty, then fill with water, drop this end to spill the water, and return to upright. The square end can rest on the barrel edge or on a rock so that the rhythmic clack is produced when it returns to its upright angle. ▼

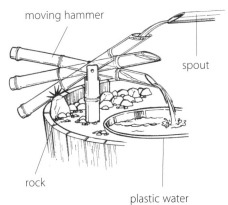

Fine-Tuning Your Fountain

▶ Step 1: Test the Fountain

A well-proportioned *Shishi Odoshi* fills and empties with a smooth, rhythmic swoosh and clack. If the hammer doesn't drop when it's full of water, trim more from its square back end. If the pointed-cup end is too heavy when empty to right itself, shorten it slightly.

You can trim the pivot pin to length when you're finished. Cut it to project about ½ inch (13 mm) beyond the side of the cradle and sand its end to a smooth bevel. Then drill a ⅛-inch (3 mm) hole through the pivot pin up against the outside of the cradle arm and drive a tiny peg through the hole to lock the pivot pin in place in the cradle. The locking peg can be cut from a tiny twig of bamboo, with a node forming the head. Sand it smooth and push it into place with your fingers.

▶ Step 2: Decorate with Plants and Stones

Plant the margin of the barrel with whatever tickles your fancy. Miniature bamboo plants and small junipers will give this fountain the simple look of a Japanese garden. To keep plantings from overwhelming and hiding the fountain, spread pea gravel or beach stones liberally on top of the potting soil. A few choice rocks carefully placed and a stone candle holder may add the finishing touches.

Half Barrel with Spouting Sculpture

This project is less demanding than many and results in an outdoor fountain with a pool deep enough to support a water lily and many marginal bog plants. It makes a good place to show off a piece of ceramic, concrete, or bronze sculpture. If the sculpture is not fitted with a tube for water, you can rig it yourself as suggested on page 68.

◄ Spouting sculptures are a classic model in traditional fountaineering. You can find them in museums, formal gardens, and backyards around the world.

channel set in sculpture

vinyl tube

half barrel reservoir

pump inside barrel

concrete block support for sculpture

pump's electrical cord

MATERIALS

The Reservoir
- Wooden half barrel
- Rigid plastic barrel liner (optional)

The Pump
- Pump, approximately 140 GPH (532 l per hour)
- GFCI outlet

Fountain Elements
- Sculpture with tubing
- Piece of $1/8''$ (3 mm) diameter soft copper tubing (optional; use if there's no tubing in sculpture)
- Assorted pieces of vinyl hose as needed to connect sculpture and pump

By setting your sculpture back into the surrounding foliage, you can hide the platform.

Preparing the Half Barrel

▶ Step 1: Make the Barrel Watertight

These barrels, originally intended for aging whiskey or wine, become watertight if they're allowed to sit for several hours full of water, which swells the wooden staves and seals the seams between them. In cool, wet climates the barrel will not leak if kept filled with water. In some very hot and dry locations, however, the outside of the staves might dry out excessively, opening the seams. One way to keep the barrel leakproof is to line it with a rigid plastic barrel liner.

▶ Step 2: Find the Right Location

The barrel will always be damp underneath, so it's only suitable for locations where some moisture will do no harm. I located mine, for example, in a corner of the garden where a backdrop of tall evergreen boxwoods meets the clapboard siding of the garage. This sheltered location gets six hours of sun per day.

> **ⓑ tip** If the sculpture you wish to use is not intended for use as a fountain piece and does not have interior tubing, you can fit copper tubing onto it yourself. See Rigging Sculpture for Fountains on page 68.

Setting Up the Fountain

▶ Step 1: Erect the Sculpture

Your sculpture will need to be raised up over the half barrel. Try setting it on a low wall, a decorative base, or a hidden platform of concrete blocks. For my fountain, I was able to conceal a pedestal made of concrete blocks stacked behind the barrel by nestling the barrel into the boxwood foliage. On this stable platform I stood the 30-pound (14 kg) concrete maiden I found in an antiques store. She was cast with a tube inside to carry water to the lip of her jar. The copper tube projects from the concrete at the back of her robe, where it's joined to flexible vinyl hose. Attach the hose to the pump, telescoping it to larger sections as required to fit the pump's outflow.

▶ Step 2: Test the Water Flow

Set the pump in the reservoir, plug it in, and adjust the flow of the water so that it doesn't splash outside the barrel. If it persists in doing so, lowering the level of water in the barrel should help keep the splash within the walls.

▶ Step 3: Add Decorative Elements

To plant the half barrel as a water garden, simply set plants in their pots at the depths recommended. Use bricks to raise them higher if necessary. See appendix A for suggestions.

Rigging Sculpture for Fountains

Dorothy Lord and her husband, Alan, are the owners of the Brass Baron, a San Diego–based company that designs and fabricates cast-brass and -bronze sculpture for gardens and fountains. Many of her figures are cast with tubing already inside; water can be piped from the pump directly to the mouth of a fish or the lip of an upturned urn. Sometimes, however, Dorothy makes a fountain from an old sculpture piece that was never intended to deliver water. Many a nubile maiden hefting a water jar to her shoulder has been fitted with a tiny copper tube so that water can seem to pour from the jar into the pool below. In this way you can use a beautiful piece of sculpture as a fountain, whether or not it was made for the purpose. The following tips reveal some of Dorothy's secrets.

You need to find a piece of sculpture that will be suitable in a fountain, and it must be sized proportionally to the reservoir it will sit in or above. Dorothy's are set in a variety of existing ponds, but you can set your sculpture in just about any reservoir — including the half barrel used in the preceding project. ▼

Fitting a Spout

If your sculpture doesn't have internal tubing for fountain use, does it lend itself to a copper tube formed to an unseen back side? If so, buy a piece of soft copper tubing as small in diameter as possible, and bend it to cling to the sculpture. Bending soft tubing is something you can easily do with your bare hands, but you must proceed with care. Grasp it with both hands, thumbs together, and gently pull the tubing around your thumbs as they push it away from you, creating an arching curve rather than a sudden sharp angle. Bend slightly and move on, then go back over the same part again to increase the curve. ▼

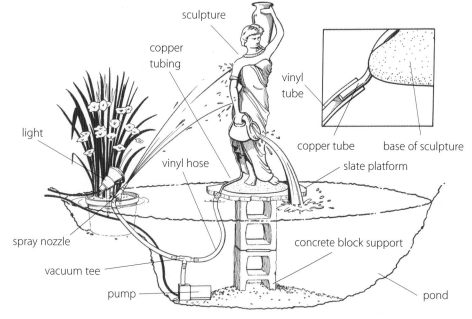

Outdoor spouting sculpture fountains can be lovely garden ornaments even through winter so long as the water is shut off before the first hard freeze. The water must also be drained from the tubing to protect it from splitting when ice forms.

For optimal water flow, gently bend copper tubing into graceful, form-fitting arches rather than sharp angles.

The danger is that you will attempt too extreme a bend in one spot, and the tubing will crimp flat. This is hard to correct. You will need to straighten the tubing and grasp it with pliers to squeeze the points of the crimp back into as close to a round shape as possible. Still, the tubing will never again be likely to bend in this spot without crimping.

Once the tubing fits the sculpture, tighten its curves slightly so that it will cling to the form and stay put.

Providing Support

In or just outside the reservoir, the sculpture needs to be supported at or near water level so it will be fully visible. In a pond, you can build a level, secure footing by setting concrete blocks on a pad of pea gravel. A slab of flagstone laid on top will make the platform more attractive. Place the art on the flagstone, set the pump in the pond, attach the hose fitted to the sculpture to the pump outflow (by adding successively larger sections of hose if necessary), and begin experimenting with the play of water on the form.

Spraying the Sculpture

Whether or not your sculpture is suitable for hidden tubing, it may benefit aesthetically from being sprayed by jets of water from a distance. Various pieces of hardware available in auto-supply

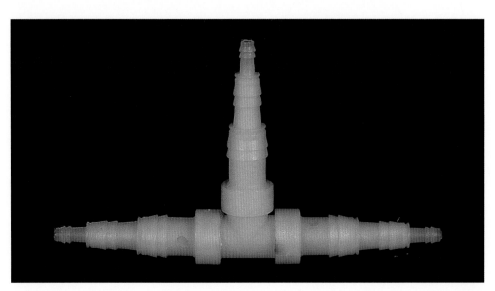

A three-armed vacuum tee will allow you to set up multiple spouts, so that you can spray your sculpture from outside jets.

stores are very helpful in this sort of endeavor. A small plastic fitting known as a vacuum tee can accomplish wonders, serving both as the spray nozzle itself and to rig up a network of tubes from the pump so that you can have more than one spray nozzle. The vacuum tee is a T-shaped coupling onto which vinyl tubing can be slid. Locking ridges on the outside of the tee keep the tubing from slipping off. The ends of the tee's three arms are tapered so that you can cut off some of the length to increase the inside diameter and, hence, the flow of water from the arm. Get yourself a handful of vacuum tees and you can create your own waterworks.

A handy place to anchor a spray nozzle is a large, stable, potted bog plant with soil near or at the surface of the water. Remember that for a pump

to create the pressure to feed two or three spraying outlets and to raise water to the top of the sculpture, it needs to be more powerful than the average fountain pump. Be sure to review The Pump and Electrical System on page 4 before buying one. In addition, you can try to get advice on capacity from the retailer from whom you buy your pump.

Lighting

A pond that features jets of water playing on a standing sculpture adapts naturally to the addition of lighting. See appendix C on page 147 for suppliers of pond lighting. These lights are water resistant, and you can place them in the same plants as the spray nozzles, washing both the sculpture and the spraying water with light from an unseen source.

The danger is that you will attempt too extreme a bend in one spot, and the tubing will crimp flat. This is hard to correct. You will need to straighten the tubing and grasp it with pliers to squeeze the points of the crimp back into as close to a round shape as possible. Still, the tubing will never again be likely to bend in this spot without crimping.

Once the tubing fits the sculpture, tighten its curves slightly so that it will cling to the form and stay put.

Providing Support

In or just outside the reservoir, the sculpture needs to be supported at or near water level so it will be fully visible. In a pond, you can build a level, secure footing by setting concrete blocks on a pad of pea gravel. A slab of flagstone laid on top will make the platform more attractive. Place the art on the flagstone, set the pump in the pond, attach the hose fitted to the sculpture to the pump outflow (by adding successively larger sections of hose if necessary), and begin experimenting with the play of water on the form.

Spraying the Sculpture

Whether or not your sculpture is suitable for hidden tubing, it may benefit aesthetically from being sprayed by jets of water from a distance. Various pieces of hardware available in auto-supply

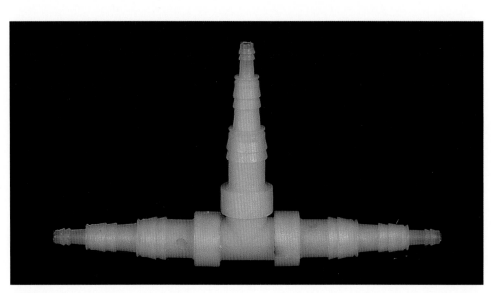

A three-armed vacuum tee will allow you to set up multiple spouts, so that you can spray your sculpture from outside jets.

stores are very helpful in this sort of endeavor. A small plastic fitting known as a vacuum tee can accomplish wonders, serving both as the spray nozzle itself and to rig up a network of tubes from the pump so that you can have more than one spray nozzle. The vacuum tee is a T-shaped coupling onto which vinyl tubing can be slid. Locking ridges on the outside of the tee keep the tubing from slipping off. The ends of the tee's three arms are tapered so that you can cut off some of the length to increase the inside diameter and, hence, the flow of water from the arm. Get yourself a handful of vacuum tees and you can create your own waterworks.

A handy place to anchor a spray nozzle is a large, stable, potted bog plant with soil near or at the surface of the water. Remember that for a pump

to create the pressure to feed two or three spraying outlets and to raise water to the top of the sculpture, it needs to be more powerful than the average fountain pump. Be sure to review The Pump and Electrical System on page 4 before buying one. In addition, you can try to get advice on capacity from the retailer from whom you buy your pump.

Lighting

A pond that features jets of water playing on a standing sculpture adapts naturally to the addition of lighting. See appendix C on page 147 for suppliers of pond lighting. These lights are water resistant, and you can place them in the same plants as the spray nozzles, washing both the sculpture and the spraying water with light from an unseen source.

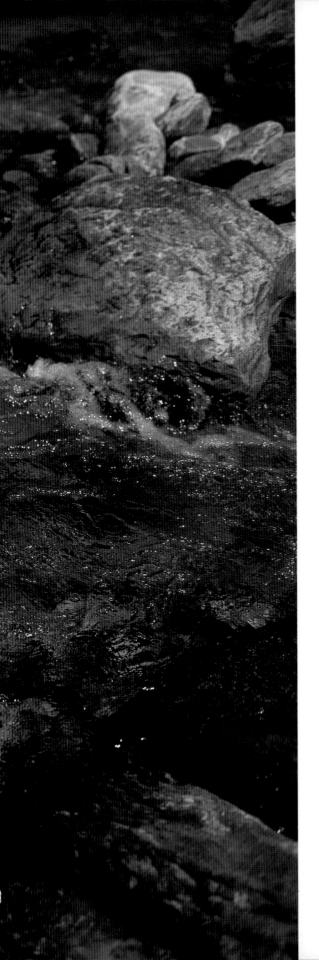

4 Projects in Ceramic, Concrete, Stone, and Metal

Because of their permanence and the beauty of their surfaces, ceramic, concrete, stone, and metal are all highly prized media for water artists. For the most part they are not absorbent or soluble, and as such all are natural partners for water.

If you're alarmed by the thought of undertaking construction with these more durable materials, take heart — with some time and patience, they're not the least bit difficult to work with, and they can offer you incredible results. If your view of concrete, for example, is limited to city streets and curbs, then consider sandcasting to produce a rough, sandy texture, or try plaster casting, which makes possible a faithful reproduction of the most subtle details. Hypertufa mixes peatmoss into the formula for a color and texture close to that of natural stone.

As with all fountain projects, remember that you, the fountainmaker, are allowed to make mistakes. After all, you can fix nearly anything by doing it over again. So relax! Concentrate on enjoying the time spent working with your hands, and allow yourself to experiment with the different construction media described here.

Small Mosaic Fountain

his indoor-outdoor fountain allows you to take advantage of found objects. There is almost no limit to the range of materials you can use in mosaic patterns. Generally, they need to be small enough to attach to the backing board and to embed in grout; they should also be impervious to water. You can use small pieces of clay shards from broken pottery, tiles, beads, coins, stones, beach glass; the list is long.

This fountain includes a combination of tiles bought from a tile company and small objects found on a beach: softly rounded beach glass, shells, pebbles. The fountain piece is provided by water falling from a small ledge in the embedded beach stones. The reservoir is formed by surrounding a plastic tub with tiled plywood.

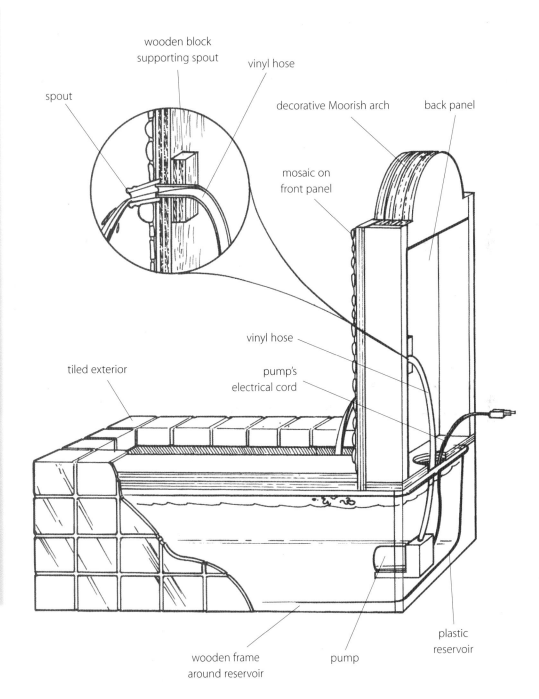

wooden block supporting spout

vinyl hose

spout

decorative Moorish arch

back panel

mosaic on front panel

vinyl hose

tiled exterior

pump's electrical cord

wooden frame around reservoir

pump

plastic reservoir

MATERIALS

Reservoir and Fountain Elements

- Small plastic storage bin or dishpan, approximately 12 x 16 x 6" (30 x 40 x 15 cm)
- 1/2" (13 mm) CDX (outdoor) plywood: 1/2 sheet, 4' x 4' (1.2 m x 1.2 m)
- 1" x 1" (2.5 x 2.5 cm) tiles: approximately 6 sq ft (1.8 sq m)
- Vinyl hose: 12" (30 cm) lengths of 1/4" and 3/8" ID (6 and 9 mm); 1/2" (30 mm) ID if pump requires

For the Pump

- Pump with flow control, 80 GPH (304 l per hour)
- GFCI outlet located near fountain site

Decorative Elements

- Collection of beach glass, shells, small beach pebbles — any objects approximately 1/4" (6 mm) in thickness

Tools

- Table saw
- 4d penny galvanized finish nails and hammer
- Wood glue
- Bandsaw, coping saw, or saber saw
- Electric drill with 1/2" and 3/8" (13 and 9 mm) bits
- Tile mastic
- Tile scoring tool
- Tile nippers
- Clear silicone caulk
- Tile grout
- Rubber spatula
- Toothbrush

Broken pieces of colorful tile, whether left over from another project or the result of a cutting "mistake" from this project, can be used to form the mosaic panel.

Planning the Layout

▶ Step 1: Choose the Reservoir

Your first step is to locate the plastic basin for the reservoir. All dimensions will be based on this all-important piece. You may find the perfect item in your supermarket being sold as a storage bin or dishpan. It needs to be rectangular or square rather than round so that you can build a wooden frame around it. Once this decision is made, you can design the rest of the fountain.

▶ Step 2: Estimate the Frame Dimensions

Assuming that you are using a 12 by 16 by 6 inch (30 by 40 by 15 cm) plastic bin, draw a box with outside dimensions of 14 inches (35 cm) wide by 18 inches (45 cm) long by 7 inches (17.5 cm) deep. This allows an additional inch — ½ inch (13 mm) for the thickness of the plywood and ½ inch of breathing room — so your pan will fit inside it.

▶ Step 3: Estimate the Back Panel and Lip Dimensions

Draw a plywood lip 2 inches (5 cm) wide around the four sides of the box. Decide which side will be the back with the mosaic surface and water spout. Now draw the back panel for the mosaic surface, extending another 14 inches (35 cm) above the lip. You'll build up the back panel around the edges to total 2 inches (5 cm) in thickness by adding strips of ½-inch (13 mm) plywood. Add strips of ½-inch by 2-inch (1.3 by 5 cm) plywood to the front and two sides of the lip around the tub to build it up to 1 inch (2.5 cm), so that you can use whole tiles on the inside face rather than cutting them. ▼

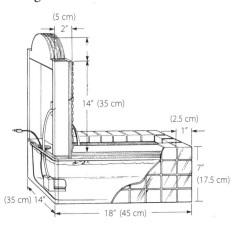

▶ Step 4: Estimate the Tile Dimensions

Having drawn your frame, your next step is to plan how you will tile it. Depending on what size tiles you select, the dimensions of your wooden frame may need to change. Planning at this stage saves a lot of time later. I am assuming that you have a source for the traditional 1-inch (2.5 cm) square ceramic tiles; failing this, plan to use larger tiles and do some cutting. You can buy these tiles with "bullnosed" (finished and rounded) edges for a finished effect wherever the tile meets on an outside corner.

Design the exact layout of the tiles on your drawing so that you can adjust the dimensions of the wooden frame, if necessary, before you build it. In this design, you'll tile all outside surfaces with flat commercial tiles, except the front of the back panel. Plan to tile vertical surfaces first (including inside the plywood lip around the top of the frame). Then lap these surfaces with tiles on the horizontal surfaces.

The front of the back panel will be finished with a circular arrangement of found objects surrounded by a border of 1-inch (2.5 cm) commercial tiles in a contrasting color. I recommend using dark blue tiles as a border around the mosaic on the back panel and around the lip of the pool, with a sand-colored tile for the sides of the pool.

> **ⓑ tip**   As you design a wood frame for the fountain, remember that there are limits to how small the frame can be, because water falling from any height will splash according to the velocity of its flow. The dimensions I give here are a guideline. The goal is to create a fountain that splashes enough that you can hear it, but not so much that it splashes water onto indoor furniture and floor.

Cutting and Assembling the Wooden Parts

▶ Step 1: Cut the Plywood Parts

Now that your frame is designed and the tiling laid out, you need to cut all the plywood parts for the frame and back panel. The best way to cut the pieces is on a table saw, which ensures square corners and straight edges. Draw the Moorish arch detail directly onto the back panel piece as soon as you've cut it.

The following list should serve as a guide. Dimensions depend on the size of your reservoir:

- 1 front of base surround
- 2 sides of base surround
- 1 back panel
- 1 front deck piece
- 2 side deck pieces
- 1 front deck build-up piece
- 2 side deck build-up pieces
- 2 pieces for framing sides of back panel to 2 inches (5 cm) thick
- 1 piece for framing bottom of back panel to 2 inches (5 cm) thick
- 3 pieces for building up top of back panel to 2 inches (5 cm) thick ▼

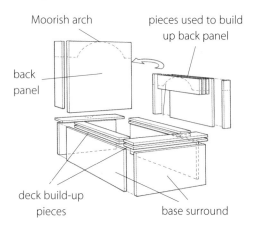

Moorish arch

pieces used to build up back panel

back panel

deck build-up pieces

base surround

▶ Step 2: Construct the Base Surround

Now, using finish nails and wood glue, assemble the base surround, as shown in the illustration at the bottom left.

▶ Step 3: Construct the Back Panel

Using finish nails and wood glue, assemble the back panel, as shown in the illustration at the bottom left. Be sure not to nail on the lines of the Moorish arch detail, where you're going to cut. Build up the thickness of the back panel behind the arched top by sandwiching together three additional pieces of ½-inch (13 mm) plywood, fastening them to the back panel to total 2 inches (5 cm) in thickness. Nail the 2-inch (5 cm) wide framing strips around the bottom and two sides of the back panel. Then cut the arch, using a bandsaw, coping saw, or saber saw. ▼

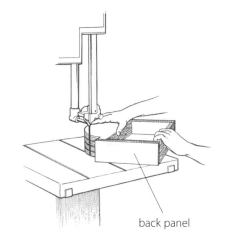

back panel

▶ Step 4: Attach the Back Panel to the Base

Set the back panel vertically on the lip of the base and screw them together. With a drill bit of at least 1 inch (2.5 cm), drill a hole for the hose and the pump's electrical cord through the area where the lip of the base surround and the bottom of the back panel assembly are joined. ▼

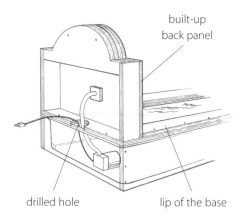

built-up back panel

drilled hole

lip of the base

▶ Step 5: Apply Tile to the Frame

Spread tile mastic over the base and the sides of the back panel one section at a time, combing it to maintain even thickness. Press the 1-inch (2.5 cm) tiles into the adhesive, butting them firmly together.

If you have miscalculated the dimensions and have to trim a tile to make it fit, first score its surface with a line you want to cut. Then nip away small pieces with the tile nippers until you reach the line. Save all good-sized broken pieces for the mosaic on the back panel.

Forming the Spout

▶ Step 1: Drill a Hole for the Spout

Now you've tiled all surfaces except the decorative back panel. First, cut a 12-inch (30 cm) length of hose of ¼-inch (6 mm) ID. Although this size of hose is probably too small to fit your pump's outflow, it allows a smaller, easier-to-conceal hole in the mosaic of the back panel. Add lengths of larger-sized hose to telescope it to the proper diameter to fit your pump.

Using a ⅜-inch (9 mm) bit, drill a hole in the center of the back panel for the hose. The hole should fit the outside diameter of the hose tightly enough that the hose stays in the hole. Then seal the edge grain of the plywood on the inside of the hole with silicone caulk.

> **ⓑ tip** For the decorative elements of the mosaic, I prefer to use clear silicone caulk, not the tile mastic used for the flat, commercial tiles. Silicone sets slowly and cannot hold anything firmly in place until it does, though, so while building, you should tilt the whole assembly onto its back to let the silicone set firmly before gravity pulls the pieces downward.

▶ Step 2: Select and Affix the Spout Piece

The spout needs a ledge of some kind to lead the water from the hose out into the air to fall freely into the basin. Select something that is smooth, slightly curved, and at least 2 inches (5 cm) long, such as the rounded lip of an old beach bottle glass or a piece of shell. Glue this into the bottom of the hole, carving out some wood to accommodate and support it. If necessary, you can fasten a small scrap of plywood to the back of the panel at this spot to make more wood to carve out and more support for this spout. ▼

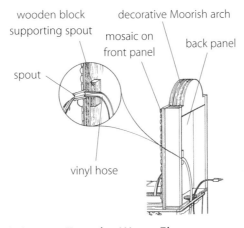

wooden block supporting spout

decorative Moorish arch

mosaic on front panel

back panel

spout

vinyl hose

▶ Step 3: Test the Water Flow

Place the hose in the spout hole, set the pump in the water, and plug it in to see how the water falls. If the water splashes excessively, you can move the hole for the hose and spout to a lower spot. Any changes now can be concealed by the small stones and beach glass you will use to make the mosaic.

Making the Mosaic

▶ Step 1: Plan the Mosaic Pattern

When the water falls the way it should, begin arranging pieces of your mosaic materials on a board or table in a pattern that pleases you. This gives you a rough guide for which pieces go in what order as you transfer them to the back panel.

▶ Step 2: Assemble the Mosaic

Glue the mosaic pieces onto the back panel. Use plenty of silicone caulk to bed them as you place them on the panel, but do not let the silicone fill the spaces between the pieces; these will be filled with grout.

As you complete the pattern of beach glass, bits of tile, shells, and small pebbles, remember to place the pieces as close to each other as possible. You'll fill the small spaces with grout, but any spaces wider than ¼ inch (6 mm) may crack from shrinkage. Arranging the pieces so that they fit together like a puzzle is the ideal. Still, if you can't avoid some larger spaces, don't worry. You can fill any cracks that form in the grout with more grout later.

When you have finished covering the back panel with mosaic, set it aside to dry thoroughly.

Applying Grout

▶ Step 1: Grout the Tile

While you are waiting for the mosaic to dry, you can apply grout to the rest of the fountain. Mix a quantity of grout with water according to the instructions on the container. Using a rubber spatula, work it into the spaces between tiles and scrape the surfaces clean. Run the handle of a toothbrush (or other small implement) over the joints to compress the grout and round the joints. As the grout dries, polish it off the tile surfaces with a sponge and old towel scraps.

▶ Step 2: Grout the Mosaic

Grouting the mosaic surface takes more patience. Before you begin, check for silicone protruding from between pieces. Trim this with a sharp knife so that the grout joints will be continuous and uninterrupted by clear silicone. Now apply grout to small areas at a time. Spread it thickly and compress it into the joints with the toothbrush handle. Wipe the excess off the uneven surface as it dries and polish with towel scraps.

Pique assiette, a technique of making mosaics from bits and pieces of broken ceramics, is another wonderful form to use in this mosaic fountain.

Finishing Touches

▶ Step 1: Finalize the Fountain Elements

Your fountain is now complete. Glue the hose to the spout hole with silicone caulk. When it's dry, fill the basin with water and drop in the pump. Attach the hose to the pump's outflow and plug the pump in to a GFCI outlet.

▶ Step 2: Add Plants and Fish

With its large pool area, this fountain can house a variety of water plants (potted or floating) and even a few small goldfish. See appendix A for some suggestions.

Working with Clay

Working with clay allows you to delve hands-on into the shape and formation of your fountain piece. However, before you get going on a clay modeling project, read through the considerations outlined here. They'll help you avoid some of the more common frustrations.

Using a Kiln

The Ceramic Spouting Wall Fountain, Splashing Ceramic Lotus Fountain, and Small Ceramic Spouting Sculpture all use clay construction for their fountain elements, and all require access to a kiln for firing the clay pieces. Before you begin firing, you should learn several things about the kiln you plan to use: What is the temperature of the firing? Which clay body will mature successfully at this temperature? Usually, the best policy is to use the same clay as the potter or ceramic artist who is already using the kiln. You should also ask how big the kiln is, and what size pieces it is able to accommodate. For example, some of the lotus leaves you may model for the Splashing Ceramic Lotus Fountain may be larger in diameter than the kiln. Be sure your pieces will fit into the kiln you plan to

use — you can expect up to 10 percent shrinkage in your clay during the initial drying period.

If you have no potter friends willing to fire your sculpture, it may be possible to enroll in a local pottery class to obtain access to a kiln. Check with art associations, continuing education programs at local universities, and craft guilds. Ceramics supply stores sometimes run studio programs. Even if they don't they're good starting points when you start asking for leads on kiln access.

Keeping It Pliable

In any ceramic project it is important to manage the drying of the clay. It should remain "leather hard" (or even softer if possible) as long as you plan to add more clay to it. Allowing the surface to become wet under its plastic covering will remove detail. Allowing it to become too dry will make it difficult to add to without cracking. The best solution is to try to finish the piece in one day. If you must store it unfinished, cover it with well-squeezed-out damp paper towels and a sheet of soft plastic, such as the bags dry cleaning is wrapped in. Tuck the plastic underneath for a tight seal and check frequently.

Scoring and Slipping

Cracking happens whenever clays of different drynesses are joined and then allowed to dry so quickly that they cannot equalize. The wetter one shrinks

more than the drier one, and they are forced to disconnect by means of a crack. Whenever you join two pieces of clay, you should use a technique known as scoring and slipping. This entails making a series of scratches in the surfaces to be bonded (scoring), then painting them with a slurry of watery clay (slip). The scratches help the two surfaces exchange water across the joint and equalize their moisture contents. Keeping the clay well covered during drying can slow the process enough to allow them to shrink at the same rate and dry without cracking.

The most basic tools for working with clay are, counterclockwise from the top: a sponge, wooden modeling tool, fettling knife, and wire trimming tool. Of course, you can always make do with a kitchen sponge, spoon, and knife.

Ceramic Spouting Wall Fountain

*B*ecause it hangs on a vertical surface, you'll most likely use the fountain in an enclosed garden setting. A stone wall or the side of a building can provide the necessary hanging surface, behind either an in-ground pool or a large whiskey barrel or trough filled with water.

Any ceramic sculpture, if porous enough, will absorb water and therefore be vulnerable to frost damage. If you live in a climate subject to winter frosts, then this fountain should be removed from the garden and stored for the winter. A more frost-hardy alternative, and also a good choice if you do not have access to a kiln for firing clay, is to cast the clay plaque in concrete (see the Concrete Spouting Wall Fountain on page 89). Because of the lengthy drying times involved, both versions of the spouting wall fountain take a few days to make.

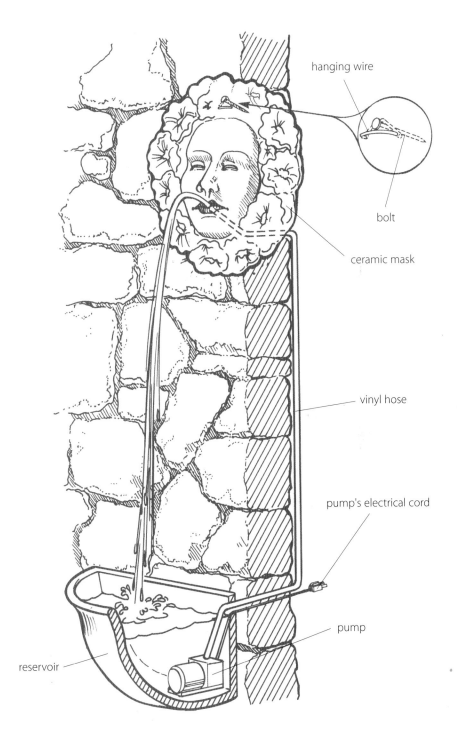

hanging wire

bolt

ceramic mask

vinyl hose

pump's electrical cord

pump

reservoir

If you don't want to make your own mask, you can also construct this fountain with a pre-molded mask purchased from your local garden center or pottery shop.

Making the Plaster Mask

▶ Step 1: Prepare the Subject

You'll begin by making a plaster mold of a person's face. A man, woman, or older child would all be fine; in this example I worked with a young woman. Have the subject lie on her back in a relaxing environment where she will be content to stay for half an hour without moving. Carefully and thoroughly coat her face and throat with a thin film of petroleum jelly. Be sure she is resting comfortably, and have her place drinking straws in her nostrils and practice breathing.

▶ Step 2: Mix the Plaster

Mix the plaster in a flexible and/or disposable container to make cleanup easier, and start with about 1½ quarts (1.5 l) of warm water. First sprinkle the plaster lightly with your fingers into the water — without stirring — until the plaster forms an island in the center and has absorbed all but a small moat of water around the island.

When you stir plaster, it's important to introduce as little air into the mix as possible. Wet one hand and slide it to the bottom of the bowl with your fingers together. Then without agitating the surface, gently squish the lumps and mix the plaster until you obtain a thick, creamy texture. You should begin to feel the plaster warm up as the setting reaction begins. Use it as soon as it begins to thicken.

▶ Step 3: Apply Plaster to the Subject's Face

When the plaster begins to warm and thicken, scoop it from the bowl in gentle handfuls and place them on your subject's nose, cheeks, forehead, and chin. Pile the plaster as thick as you can on these upper areas, patting it to help it slump around the nose and lips (no laughing!). Settle the mass of plaster over the chin and throat, trying to keep it at least 1 inch (2.5 cm) thick. As it sets, it becomes warmer. Have the subject wait until it is firm before she sits up, allowing gravity to release it from her skin. The plaster mold will become more absorbent as it dries, so give it a day or two before you use it.

▼ You may soon find your fountain visited by small creatures such as toads and dragonflies.

Molding the Clay Mask

▶ Step 1: Roll Out a Clay Slab

Now that you have a plaster mold of a face (the "negative"), you can begin to construct the clay wall plaque (the "positive") that will spout water into your pond or basin. Pat a lump the size of a large orange into a ball. On a sheet of canvas or heavy cloth about 18 inches (45 cm) square, flatten the ball by repeatedly pounding it with your fist and turning it over so that it doesn't stick. The clay should be soft enough to work easily, and dry enough not to stick to the cloth. Continue this flattening and flipping until the slab is about 1 inch (2.5 cm) thick and only slightly larger in diameter than the plaster face.

⑥ tip For a smoother surface, finish rolling out the clay slab with a rolling pin or wine bottle.

▶ Step 2: Lay the Clay Slab in the Plaster Mold

When the clay slab is ready, carefully lay it into the plaster mold, smoothest-side down. Cup it into the mold so that the clay remains thick as you press it into the facial features. Do this gently and thoroughly, being sure to apply enough pressure to force it into all hollows. Stroke the inside surface with your fingers or a spoon. When you feel that you've finished, leave the mold for a few hours to dry. ▼

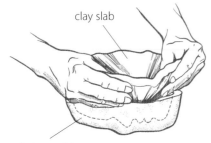

clay slab

plaster mold

> **tip** If the clay becomes thicker than 1 inch (2.5 cm) at the upper edges of the mold, where it is compressed, carve some away with the spoon. If it seems to have stretched thin in the bottom, add more clay to any problem areas.

▶ Step 3: Remove the Clay Face from the Mold

The plaster will absorb water from the clay, drying it quickly and shrinking the clay face as it does so. When you can see that the face has shrunk away from the mold, turn the whole thing over in your hands to see if gravity will help the clay face drop from the mold as you gently pull on the edges to loosen it. Don't worry if you have to distort the shape a little to do this; you can easily reshape it. If it proves stubborn, wait for more shrinkage. When you are satisfied with the mask, set it aside, wrapped in plastic to keep it soft.

> **tip** As always, relax. The worst thing that can happen is that you will mess up one or two faces before you get the hang of it and produce a good one.

Forming the Plaque

▶ Step 1: Roll Out the Clay Plaque

On a plywood board approximately 24 inches (60 cm) square, covered with the sheet of heavy cloth, roll out a large slab of clay to ½ inch (13 mm) thickness and approximately 14 inches (35 cm) in diameter. After the clay finishes shrinking during drying and firing, the diameter will be diminished by approximately 15 percent, or almost 2 inches (5 cm), to a finished diameter of 12 inches (30 cm).

▶ Step 2: Trim the Plaque

Letting the outline be somewhat uneven, trim the clay slab with your fettling knife to an oval that will frame the outer dimensions of the face. Trim the edge of the face so that it sits flat, then set it in place on the plaque. Mark the outline, remove the face, and cut out the plaque so that only ½ inch (13 mm) of clay remains around the inside of the outline. ▼

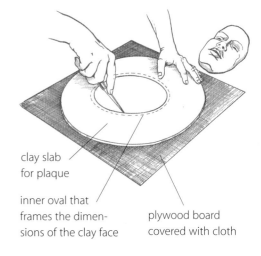

clay slab for plaque

inner oval that frames the dimensions of the clay face

plywood board covered with cloth

▶ Step 3: Join the Mask to the Plaque

Heavily score the inner band of the plaque and the back edge of the face, then daub them both with slip (very soft clay). (See Working with Clay on page 79 for instruction in this technique.) Set the face on the plaque and wiggle it while pressing down so that slip is squeezed from the joint all the way around. Wipe this away with your sponge. Roll a thin coil of clay and lay it around the joint, then press it into the joint and smooth it to round the junction between face and wall plaque. Then cover the clay form with a plastic sheet to keep the clay soft and malleable, and set it aside to begin to dry.

▶ Step 4: Smooth the Joint from Inside

When the slab is dry enough that you can lift it by means of its backing cloth, peel away the cloth. Hold the soft clay form in your hand or set it in a box of soft rags for support, then scrape off any protruding clay on the interior. Compress the joint from inside by smoothing it with the spoon or a rib. Remember, most scrapes and dents caused by this process can be fixed later. If you have a helper, this is a good time to get assistance.

▶ Step 5: Make a Hole for the Spout

Insert the tip of a fettling knife or pencil between the lips of the mask and twirl to make a small hole, about ⅛ inch (3 mm), for the spout. Form a small collar of clay, approximately ¼ inch (6 mm) thick, ½ inch (13 mm) in inside diameter, and ½ inch (13 mm) long, to fit just inside the mouth opening. Join this carefully to the mask by scoring and slipping; reinforce the joint with a narrow coil of clay around the outside of the collar. ▼

box of soft rags for support

upside-down mask   hole and collar for spout

▶ Step 6: Decorate the Frame

Lay the plaque on the plywood board. Begin adding sculptural elements — flowers, grape leaves, clusters of fruit, and/or vines — to the frame around the face, modeled from the same clay that you used for the face and plaque. Remember, no one element of this relief sculpture needs to stand alone as a perfect piece of art. Just keep adding more, and in the ultimate rich texture of natural forms they will visually reinforce each other.

▶ Step 7: Insert a Hanging Loop

The plaque will be hung by a loop of strong cord or wire. Lift the plaque and from the front make a pair of small holes by twisting a fettling knife or pencil through the plaque. Then from the back, finish the holes until they are clean, round, and more than big enough for the wire or cord you plan to use. The holes should be 1 inch (2.5 cm) apart, centered near the top edge of the frame. ▼

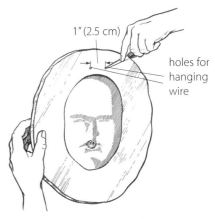

1″ (2.5 cm)

holes for hanging wire

> **ⓑ tip** On the front of the plaque, you can conceal the area between the holes, where the hanging loop will pass, beneath an overhang of leaves so that the wire or cord does not show excessively.

Drying and Firing
the Plaque

▶ Step 1: Allow the Plaque
to Air-Dry

When the plaque is complete, you can begin to allow it to dry out somewhat. Remember to check it frequently. If you see a crack beginning, gently score it, work stiff clay into the crack to repair it, then cover it tightly with dampened paper towels for several days.

When the clay seems dry, allow it to sit uncovered in hot sun or in a warm place for a day or two. The plaque must be absolutely dry before you fire it. Any coolness to touch indicates moisture, which will expand and break the clay during firing. An extra dose of care at this stage is well worth the time.

▶ Step 2: Fire the Plaque

When it is dry, bring the plaque to a kiln for firing. For an interesting finish, first bisque-fire the clay. Next brush on a dark ceramic stain or iron oxide, sponge it off while leaving some in the hollows of your sculpture, and fire the clay to maturity. This will add emphasis to the textures and will not wash off in years of outdoor use.

Setting Up the Fountain

▶ Step 1: Prepare the Plaque

To set up your fountain, insert the cord or wire through the holes in the plaque and form a loop large enough to fit over whatever bolt or peg you plan to use for hanging it. Hang the plaque on the wall above your pool.

Fit a length of tubing from the pump to the plaque, telescoping pieces of different diameter where required. Generally, the best size for the main body of the run is the smallest diameter you'll be using; this is better able to curve around obstructions without flattening where bent, easier to hide, and less expensive. If you cannot make the tubing stay firmly enough in the collar behind the plaque, fasten it with epoxy putty or silicone caulk.

▶ Step 2: Test the Water Flow

Drop the pump into the water, attach it to the tubing, and plug it in to see if the water flows as you hoped. You may need to make alterations. If the water does not flow strongly enough to reach the mouth, you may be able to adjust the pump's flow control or lower your plaque to correct this.

For added effect, surround your mask with foliage that resembles the leaves and vines you've molded into the back plaque.

Working with Concrete

Tim Nojaim is a stone carver, mold maker, and maker of cast-stone sculpture. He operates his one-man studio in Alexandria, Virginia, hand carving stone for mantelpieces and church spires, as he was trained to do during an Italian apprenticeship. He is also a talented creator of rubber molds for concrete production and has extensively advised both me and my partner, Bob Adams, in mold making and casting concrete sculpture.

Following is Tim's recipe for making concrete and matching stucco mixes. The ingredients are available in most garden centers and building supply shops.

Mixing Your Own Concrete

Premixed concrete is easy to buy in any hardware store. Although it's convenient, its dark gray color and large gravel aggregate are better suited to porch steps than to sculpture. If you are able to buy the ingredients separately and wish to mix your own, here is Tim's "from scratch" recipe for a light gray concrete that looks more like real stone. I usually use a 1-quart (1 l) plastic container for a measuring scoop.

Make-Your-Own Concrete Recipe

- 1 part white cement
- 1 part gray cement
- 5 parts sand
- About 1 part water (the amount varies with humidity and dampness of sand)

1. Mix together the cement and sand.
2. Slowly and gently stir in the water, bit by bit. Too much water will weaken the final product; too little will result in a finished piece full of air bubbles. Try to keep the mix as dry as possible, while taking care to wet all of it evenly. You should be able to see a shine on the surface if you smooth it with a trowel, but it should be a stiff mix.

Although you cannot avoid introducing air bubbles, with care you can minimize their presence. You then must rely on tamping after you pack the mix into the mold to get them out.

Mixing Your Own Stucco

Tim also has a recipe for a stucco mix useful for filling air bubbles. Mix it in small amounts as needed — a tablespoon (5 ml) is probably a good measuring scoop to start with.

Make-Your-Own Stucco Recipe

- 2 parts gray cement
- 3 parts white cement
- 5 parts sifted sand
- Water (the amount varies with humidity and dampness of sand)

1. Sift all the sand and cement through a window screen or fine sieve.
2. Combine the dry mixture with enough water to produce a thick paste.

▼ The Birdshower Fountain (page 111) uses a handcast concrete basin as a reservoir.

Concrete Spouting Wall Fountain

Perhaps you want to create the Nymphaeum (the Ceramic Wall Fountain), described on page 81, but you have no garden pool and no available firing facilities to make a ceramic plaque. The following variation shows you how to cast the plaque in concrete. Because concrete is more resistant to damage than ceramic when temperatures drop below freezing, this is also a good wall fountain for those who live in colder northern climates. It uses for its water reservoir not an in-ground pool, but an antique soapstone sink, which you can often find in junk shops. Alternatively, a half whiskey barrel or other appropriately sized container can be used.

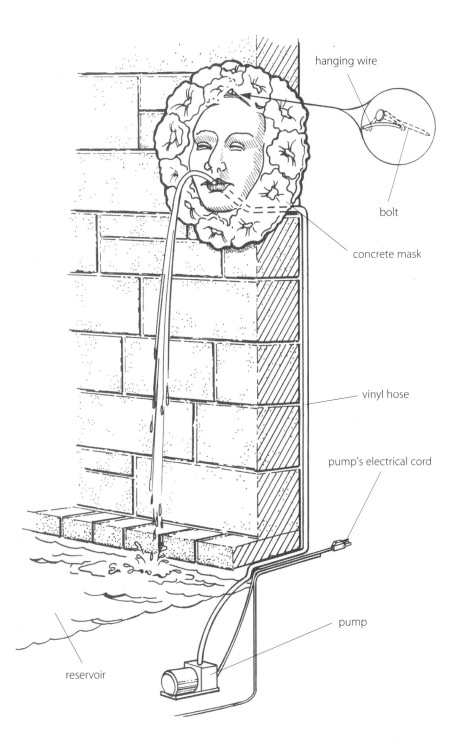

hanging wire

bolt

concrete mask

vinyl hose

pump's electrical cord

pump

reservoir

Materials

For the Reservoir
- Soapstone sink (or other reservoir of similar size)

For the Pump
- Pump, 140 GPH (532 l per hour)
- GFCI outdoor outlet or extension cord

Fountain Elements
- 50 pounds (22.7 kg) plaster of Paris
- 15 pounds (6.8 kg) clay, any type
- 2¹⁄₂″ (6.25 cm) wide wood strips: 8–10′ (2.4–3 m)
- ¹⁄₄″ (6 mm) ID vinyl hose: 4–5′ (1.2–1.5 m), plus short lengths of larger sizes for telescoping (if needed)
- 25 pounds (11.4 kg) premixed cement-gravel mixture (or see page 87 to mix your own)
- 2 x 4 lumber: 8′ (2.4 m)
- 6″ (15 cm) strong copper wire

Tools
- Petroleum jelly
- Plastic dishpan of clean water
- 2 drinking straws
- 18″ (45 cm) square sheet of canvas
- Rolling pin or wine bottle
- Large metal spoon with strong handle
- Sheet of lightweight plastic
- Large square of unfinished plywood
- Clay-working tools: fettling knife, loop-style trimming tool, wooden modeling tool, sponge
- Hammer
- Nails
- Spray wax, for a mold-release agent
- Electric drill with ¹⁄₄″ (6 mm) bit
- Chopstick or ¹⁄₄″ (6 mm) dowel
- Block of wood
- Trowel or kitchen knife
- Chisel or screwdriver
- Pliers
- Handheld grinder or rasp
- Strainer or window screen

Constructing the Clay Mold

▶ Step 1: Model the Plaster and Clay Masks

The wall plaque for this fountain is constructed in exactly the same manner as that of the Ceramic Spouting Wall Fountain, except the wall plaque you end up with will be a concrete casting of that clay plaque.

Turn back to the Ceramic Spouting Wall Fountain project and follow the instructions for all of the steps in Making a Plaster Mask and Molding the Clay Mask, as well as steps 1, 2, and 3 of Forming the Plaque (see pages 83–85).

▶ Step 2: Frame the Backing Board

Cut the 2½-inch (6.25 cm) wide wooden strips to 24 inches (60 cm) — the length of the sides of the unfinished plywood board. Nail or screw the strips to the edge of the plywood, forming a frame that projects at least 2 inches (5 cm) above the surface of the board. This will contain the plaster for the second mold you will make. Seal all joints of the wooden frame with clay. ▼

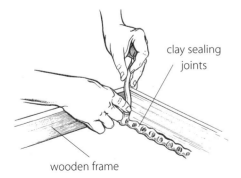

clay sealing joints

wooden frame

▶ Step 3: Add Decorative Elements to the Plaque

Lay the plaque in the plywood frame. Begin adding sculptural elements around the face to form an attractive frame for it. These can be modeled from the same clay that you used for the face and back plate. Frame the face with flowers, grape leaves, vines, and/or clusters of fruit. Relax and assure yourself that no single element of this relief sculpture needs to stand alone as a perfect piece of art. Just keep adding more, and the ultimate rich texture of natural forms will visually reinforce each other.

▶ Step 4: Prepare the Clay Plaque for the Plaster Cast

If you can, lift the completed plaque from the board, wet the board and reposition the plaque, pressing down to stick it to the wood. Examine the decorative details and the edge of the plaque itself to find any overhanging areas, and smooth them away or fill them in. This soft clay "positive" will need to be able to drop out of the rigid plaster "negative." When this is done, seal the plaque by running a modeling tool or knife around the edge so that plaster will not seep underneath it. Thoroughly coat the clay plaque and plywood box with spray wax, using several light coats so as not to wet the clay excessively.

Making the Plaster Mold

▶ Step 1: Mix the Plaster

Mix the plaster in a flexible and/or disposable container to make cleanup easier, and start with about 3 quarts (3 l) of warm water. First sprinkle the plaster lightly with your fingers into the water — without stirring — until the plaster forms an island in the center and has absorbed all but a small moat of water around the island.

Wet one hand and slide it to the bottom of the bowl with your fingers together. Then without agitating the surface, gently squish the lumps and mix the plaster until you obtain a thick, creamy texture. You should begin to feel the plaster warm up as the setting reaction begins. Use it as soon as it begins to thicken.

tip When you stir plaster, it's important to introduce as little air into the mix as possible. Be patient, and work through the mixture slowly and gently.

▶ Step 2: Pouring the Plaster

When the plaster begins to warm and thicken, gently pour it over the clay plaque in the plywood frame. Try not to introduce air bubbles as you do this. Pour enough wet plaster to cover the clay plaque with at least 1 inch (2.5 cm) thickness in all parts. If you didn't mix enough plaster in the first batch, mix more and add a second layer to the mold. When the plaque is completely covered, tap the frame of the mold gently with a hammer to encourage air bubbles to escape. ▼

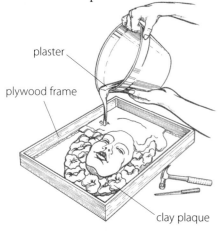

plaster

plywood frame

clay plaque

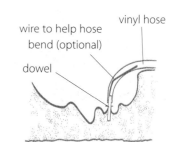

tip Try not to introduce air bubbles as you pour the plaster. Pour it smoothly and evenly, keeping the container just above the lip of the mold. Do not pour or drop the plaster in from any height, as this will splash and create air pockets.

▶ Step 3: Remove the Plaster Mold

Let the mold set until hard, perhaps 30 minutes, then gently remove it from the framed backing board. You may need to remove some of the frame in order to do so. When this is removed from the frame and emptied of clay, examine it for imperfections such as bubbles. You can fill these with soft clay just before you cast the concrete.

▶ Step 4: Build a Support Frame for the Mold

Build a rough frame of 2 x 4 lumber, about 12 to 14 inches (30 to 35 cm) square, or large enough to support your plaster mold. Set the mold on top of the frame with its deepest center part down inside it. Use wads of clay to shim it perfectly level, then spray the interior of the mold with several layers of spray wax.

▶ Step 5: Insert the Hose

With a ¼-inch (6 mm) bit, drill a hole in the mold between the lips of the face. Cut a 1-inch (2.5 cm) piece of chopstick or ¼-inch (6 mm) dowel. Grease the stick well with petroleum jelly, then insert it about halfway through this hole.

Now cut a piece of ¼-inch (6 mm) ID hose. Fit one end over the greased stick and run the rest over the bottom edge of the mold. Hold back the hose about ⅛ inch (3 mm) from the surface of the face. The idea is that the hose will be cast into the concrete to carry water from the pump to the hole between the lips, but it won't show on the surface of the face. ▼

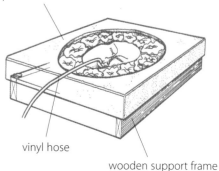

plaster mold

vinyl hose

wooden support frame

wire to help hose bend (optional)

vinyl hose

dowel

Casting the Concrete Wall Plaque

▶ Step 1: Mix the Cement

Carefully stir the water into the dry cement mixture. (If you're mixing your own, first mix the cement with the sand.) See Working with Concrete on page 87 for tips and techniques.

▶ Step 2: Fill the Mold

Pour water over the plaster mold and its frame so that it is thoroughly wet, then pour off any standing water. Scoop small amounts of concrete into the mold, tamping the concrete in carefully with a dowel or block. Lift the vinyl hose so that it emerges from the concrete at a position about even with the chin, and slightly away from the edge of the plaque. Add concrete and tamp until the mold is full. Smooth the surface with a trowel or kitchen knife. ▼

▶ Step 3: Insert the Wire Loop

Take the 6-inch (15 cm) length of copper wire, double it in half, and twist the ends together, spreading them apart below the twist. Make the loop at least an inch (2.5 cm) wide and set the wire into the wet concrete with the loop emerging from the surface near the top of your plaque. This will be the means by which you hang the plaque. Be sure the wire loop is large enough for whatever bolt or dowel you plan to hang it with.

▶ Step 4: Test the Concrete

Let the concrete casting sit for about 48 hours before you test it to determine if it's dry enough to remove the mold. To test its readiness, scrape the surface of the concrete with a metal tool. If it scratches easily, wait another half day or so. When it seems difficult to scratch, it is time to remove the mold.

▶ Step 5: Remove the Plaster Mold

The process of breaking the plaster mold away from the concrete casting is a delicate one. Concrete becomes stronger as it cures. This means that any scraping or trimming of the finished product will become increasingly difficult with time, but for the same reason, the casting will be most fragile when it first emerges from the mold.

Turn the mold over onto a board, flat-side down. Place the tip of a chisel or large screwdriver against the outer corner of the plaster and strike it with a hammer. Continue gently until the plaster cracks apart and can be removed from the concrete. By gently chipping, you can lift off all the plaster. You will eventually be left with the concrete sculpture. ▼

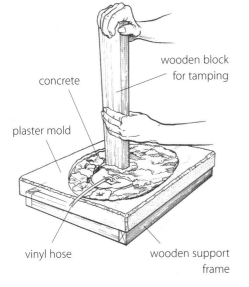

concrete

plaster mold

vinyl hose

wooden block for tamping

wooden support frame

plaster mold encasing concrete casting

Step 6: Smooth the Concrete Mold

Pull the greased wooden peg from the hole between the lips with pliers, and scrape any rough edges smooth with a screwdriver or other metal tool. If you have a handheld grinder, use it to smooth rough edges of concrete. Otherwise, a rasp works well.

The finished sculpture may have a few air bubbles that need to be filled with stucco. To make stucco that matches your premixed concrete mix, sift the dry mix through a strainer or window screen to remove coarse gravel aggregate and lumps of cement. The finer the screen, the better. Mix the resulting powder with enough water to make a paste and rub it into the holes after thoroughly soaking the sculpture in water. Smooth the surface with a damp rag and let it dry.

If you used the "from-scratch" concrete recipe, use the accompanying stucco recipe (on page 87) to match it.

Step 7: Add an Aged Finish

You can leave the concrete in its natural state or stain it to approximate the sooty look of old stone. My own preference is to stain it lightly by the following procedure:

1. Select an exterior latex paint in a dark gray color with a slight hint of green.

2. Thin it with water to a milky consistency.

3. Apply it with a brush then wipe it off with water and a rag until the paint remains only in the crevices and emphasizes the forms. Rinse with a garden hose to remove smears. Let dry.

4. Repeat this process until you obtain your desired depth of color.

Setting Up Your Fountain

Step 1: Hang the Plaque

Hang the plaque on a bolt or peg set in the wall above your reservoir. Construct a length of hose to run from your pump to the plaque, telescoping pieces of different diameters where required. Generally, the best size for the main body of the run is the smallest diameter you'll be using; this is better able to curve around obstructions without flattening where bent, easier to hide, and less expensive.

Step 2: Test the Water Flow

Drop the pump into the water, attach it to the tubing, and plug it in to see if the water flows as you hoped. You may need to make alterations. If the water does not flow strongly enough to reach the mouth, you may be able to adjust the pump's flow control or lower your plaque to correct this.

▶ This elegant lineup of spouting wall fountains can be found in Longwood Gardens (Kennett Square, Pennsylvania).

Splashing Ceramic Lotus Fountain

This project creates a ceramic lotus plant several feet high for an existing pond or pool. A submerged pump carries water to one of the distinctive flower heads, from which it falls onto one and then to another of the big saucer-shaped leaves. Because it is large and usually causes a fairly wide splash pattern, this fountain is best used outdoors, although a pool created in an atrium or greenhouse could house such a work.

The design for this fountain was created by Shirley Sheldon, who lives in the small village of Saunderstown, Rhode Island. Shirly is an artist in several media, and she enjoys designing fountains as a natural outlet for her gardening passion. Versions of the lotus fountain described here can be found in her own garden pond, as can the spouting wall fountains featured on pages 81 and 89.

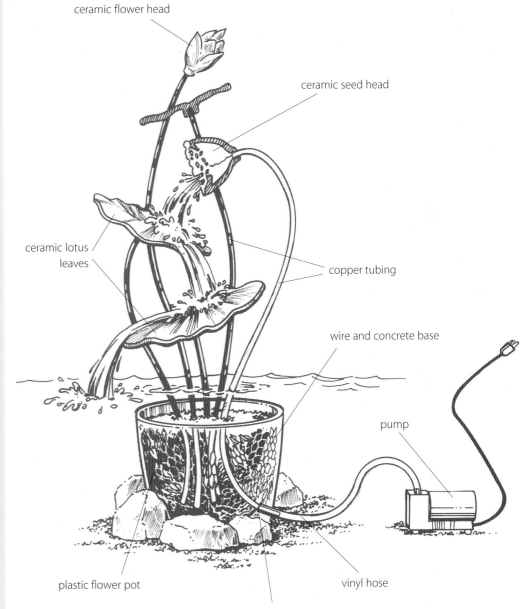

ceramic flower head

ceramic seed head

ceramic lotus leaves

copper tubing

wire and concrete base

pump

plastic flower pot

hole cut for vinyl hose

vinyl hose

For the Reservoir
- Existing pond, pool, or half barrel

For the Pump
- Pump, approximately 140 GPH (532 l per hour)
- GFCI outlet installed close to pond

Fountain Elements
- 3–5 ceramic lotus leaves in a variety of sizes (see Modeling the Lotus Plant on pages 102–103)
- 1 ceramic lotus seed head (see Modeling the Lotus Plant on pages 102–103)
- 2–3 ceramic lotus flower heads, both unopened buds and spent heads that have dropped their petals (see Modeling the Lotus Plant on pages 102–103)
- ³/₄" (9 mm) OD soft copper tubing (for leaf stems): 12–15' (3.7–4.6 m).
- ¹/₄" (6 mm) OD copper tubing (for small bud stems): 8–10' (2.4–3 m)
- Latex paint, blue-green verdigris color
- Plastic flower pot, 8–10" (20–25 cm) wide, 6–8" (15–20 cm) deep
- Wire mesh: 2–3 sq ft (0.18–0.27 sq m) (chicken wire is best)
- Clear vinyl hose: 3–6' (9.0–1.8 m) of ¹/₄" (6 mm) ID, or sized to fit copper tube
- Clear vinyl hose: 12" (30 cm) pieces of succeedingly larger ID until hose fits pump outflow
- 10–20 pounds (4.5–9 kg) premixed concrete mix (be sure it's fresh and dry)

Tools
- Fine sandpaper
- Duct tape or masking tape
- Two part epoxy putty

Many cultures believe the sacred lotus to embody qualities of inner peace and stillness. You can create your own quiet, meditative spot in the garden with the lotus fountain.

Preparing the Pieces

▶ **Step 1: Plan the Layout and Design**

With the size of your pool in mind, sketch the fountain you want to make. You will probably start with a large leaf just above the surface of the water. Arrange two to four more leaves above this in ever smaller sizes. To top them off, plan for at least three flower heads: one the spent seedhead, showing a rosette of round holes; the others smaller (and therefore higher in the air), unopened buds. Indicate the sizes of the leaves and their height above the water. Measure the depth of the pond where the lotus is to sit and draw the stems underwater, terminating in a plastic planter filled with concrete.

▶ **Step 2: Paint the Clay**

You'll want to finish the ceramic lotus pieces so that they resemble weathered bronze. Buy an exterior grade of grayish blue-green latex paint. Study the verdigris patina on copper roofing — this is the color you're aiming for.

The paint can be brushed or wiped on. In either case, you should wipe most of it off to produce the thin, irregular look of patina on metal. Don't be dismayed if you do not at first produce the look you're after. Keep working at it, perhaps adding another color on top of the first and, again, wiping most of it off. When you are satisfied, allow the finish to dry thoroughly before you put the fountain into service.

tip A dark brown paint applied over the blue-green, thinned and almost fully wiped off, gives an antique look by emphasizing the textures of petals and veins.

The lotus fountain can be found in infinite forms. This version has a greater number of smaller, flatter leaves.

Arranging the Pieces in the Base

▶ Step 3: Attach the Stems

Cut lengths of ⅜- or ¼-inch (9 or 6 mm) copper tubing and be sure they fit into the collars on the backs of your leaves and buds. These will be glued later but, for now, leave them loose. If a stem does not fit into a collar, you can whittle a wooden peg to fit inside each part and serve as a splice. Alternatively, the copper can be crushed slightly with pliers to make it fit into a tight clay collar. Be gentle with the clay; it breaks easily. When the stems are cut to length, clean them with fine sandpaper or your kitchen scouring pad and finish them to match the leaves.

▶ Step 1: Prepare the Base

All the stems will spring from a weighted base made from a concrete-filled plastic pot. Start with a plastic flower pot, 8 to 10 inches (20 to 25 cm) wide and 6 to 8 inches (15 to 20 cm) deep. The strength of this pot is not critical, since the concrete within will be the structural element. Loosely ball up enough chicken wire to fill the pot and push it in, keeping it below the rim of the pot. This will support the stems when you pour concrete around them.

Select a size of vinyl hose large enough to fit tightly over the copper tubing stem of the seed head that will deliver water; this will probably be ⅜-inch (9 mm) ID, since the copper is ⅜-inch OD. Take a long piece of this, perhaps 6 feet (1.8 m), and run the end through a hole cut low down on the side of the pot, sealing around it with tape or clay. Seal all drainage holes with tape or plastic film to seal off all escape routes for concrete. ▼

▶ Step 2: Arrange the Copper Stems

Now arrange the copper stems in the wire-filled pot. Place the stems without the leaves and flower heads on them, or else they'll be top-heavy and will tip over. The stem for the water-carrying spent seed head should be inserted into the vinyl hose. The copper tubing can be bent into graceful curves, but this must be done very carefully so as not to crimp the copper. Grasp the tubing between your hands and bend it only slightly before moving it sideways and bending it slightly again. ▼

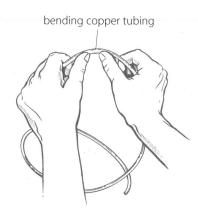

bending copper tubing

By jamming the chicken wire down more tightly around the stems for support, and by fitting the leaves and flower heads temporarily onto the stems for placement, you should be able to estimate attractive angles for the stems and arrange them accordingly.

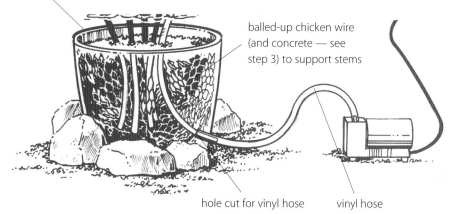

plastic flower pot

balled-up chicken wire (and concrete — see step 3) to support stems

hole cut for vinyl hose

vinyl hose

Fine-Tuning and Installation

▶ Step 3: Pour the Concrete

In another plastic pan, mix about 10 pounds (4.5 kg) of premixed concrete as directed on the bag. When this is thoroughly wetted, pour it into the pot, submerging the chicken wire and bottoms of the copper stems. Fill the pot completely — mix another batch of concrete if necessary. Try to keep the stems in their positions, but if they move slightly, don't worry — you can add more gentle curves later to enhance the grace of the finished plant.

Let the concrete cure for two to three days before putting any stress on the stems. If there are any drips or globs you hope to scrape off your base, this will be far easier within the first 12 hours than it will be later.

▶ Step 4: Affix the Ceramic Pieces

After 24 hours, you can begin to gently affix the ceramic pieces to their copper stems. Again, do not attempt to bend or adjust the stems yet — the concrete needs another day or two to set. Mixing small quantities of epoxy putty at a time, glue the seedpod, flower buds, and leaves onto the stems.

The giant lotus leaves can be laid singly in the garden as well, serving as decorative caches for rainwater.

▶ Step 1: Test the Water Flow

When the concrete has cured for a few days, test your fountain in a waterproof location, such as a bathtub or the kitchen sink. Fit the pump to the hose, if necessary adding successive sections of larger hose to telescope onto the one embedded in the concrete base (see page 102). Place the pump underwater, then plug it in and see if water falls properly from the spent seed head to one of the leaves, cascading from leaf to leaf. You may need to adjust the arrangement by carefully bending the copper stems to achieve this. Adjust the flow control on your pump to produce the correct volume of falling water.

▶ Step 2: Install the Fountain

At last your lotus should be ready to install in the location you have chosen. Lower it gently into the pond, using rocks to stabilize its base. Plug the pump into a GFCI outlet or extension cord, and enjoy the soothing sound of water tinkling from the softly rounded shapes of your lotus.

tip Any ceramic sculpture, if porous enough, will absorb water and therefore be vulnerable to frost damage. If you live in northern regions, this fountain should always be removed from the pond and stored for the winter.

Modeling the Lotus Plant

To model the lotus plant, whether for your own fountain design or for the Splashing Ceramic Lotus Fountain, you will need to cut lotus plant parts from a pond, which will probably require obtaining permission. Although these breathtaking plants are exotic, an owner of an established lotus plantation will no doubt feel that a few leaves and flower buds could be spared, because the lotus has a habit of quickly filling any water reservoir it occupies. Avoid damaging any individual plant by selecting leaves and buds from different lotuses. Leaves and immature buds are collected in midsummer, while the exotic seedpod that you'll use as a fountainhead must be collected later, after it has swelled to full fist size, in autumn. If you're lucky, a few pods may remain from the previous season for harvest in midsummer.

Be sure also to first sketch out your fountain so you'll know how many lotus parts you'll need, and how big they should be, and review Working with Clay on page 79 for tips and techniques.

Modeling the Leaves
Place an inverted plastic trash can lid either on the can itself or on a work-bench, and pour into it a pile of sand large enough to surround the ultimate clay leaf. Form a slight hollow in the center, then cover the sand with thin plastic to keep it from sticking to the clay.

Form a ball of clay and pound it on a square of canvas with your fist to flatten it. Using a rolling pin and flipping it several times to release it from the canvas, gently roll it into a slab about the same size as the leaf and ½ inch (1.3 cm) thick.

Now lay the actual leaf on the clay, with its heavily veined bottom side down, and the stem neatly sliced off. Gently and methodically, press the leaf into the wet clay. With the palm of your hand, stroke along the veins to be sure they are well indented. When you are sure the pattern has been transferred, trim the clay around the outline of the leaf, leaving the leaf on the clay, and smooth the cut edge with wet fingers.

Now pick up the clay and leaf. You may leave the canvas on, or peel it away to use on the next leaf. Without turning the arrangement over — it should remain leaf-side up — transfer it to the plastic-covered sand mold, then peel away the leaf.

When the leaf is stiff enough to handle without damage (a few hours), gently remove it from the sand by lifting the plastic or the clay itself. Re-form the sand mold so that it is slightly humped in the center and will support the leaf upside down. Replacing the plastic, position the leaf veined-side down on the mold and score the center where the stem will join it.

Now roll a thick, short coil of clay, bend it to form a loop, and join it to the back of the leaf by scoring and slipping (see Working with Clay on page 79). This collar needs to accept ⅜-inch (9 mm) copper tubing. Be sure it's a loose fit, since the clay will shrink. Add another, thinner coil around this one to reinforce it, smoothing all joints with a modeling tool and your fingers.

Cover the completed leaf with damp paper towels and plastic to dry slowly.

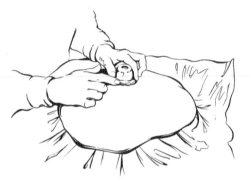

The completed collar should be about 1 inch (2.5 cm) deep and have thick, tapering walls for strength.

Modeling the Seed Heads
Pat a lump of clay about the size of your fist into a smooth ball. While turning it in your hand, begin pinching a hole in the ball's center between the thumb and fingers of one hand. Keep turning and pinching gently until you have made a well in the center, forming a thick-walled pot with a bottom only ½ to ¾ inch (13 to 19 mm) thick. Continue

pinching up the walls until they are the same thickness as the bottom and the diameter of the pot is roughly 3 inches (7.5 cm). This is called the pinch-pot method of forming pottery. The pinch pot will form the walls and stem end of the seed head.

With the tip of a fettling knife or a pencil, work a hole into the center of the bottom of the pot. Insert the ⅜-inch (9 mm) copper tubing and, by scoring and slipping, add a collar of clay about ½ inch (13 mm) long to lengthen this channel, thus strengthening it. Then remove the copper tubing. While the clay of the pot is soft, roll a ½-inch (13 mm) thick slab 3 inches (7.5 cm) in diameter, and add it to the pinch pot as a lid by scoring and slipping the edges together.

Now, copying the seedpod you have collected, model the surface with holes by twisting a fettling knife. Make these holes neat and about ¼ inch (6 mm) in diameter.

Score the edge of pot and lid, add slip, and mold them together to form the seed head.

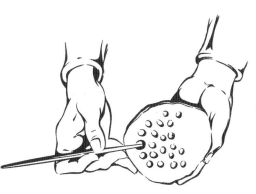

The holes will serve as water channels when the seedpod functions as the "shower head" for your fountain.

Finish any final modeling necessary to make your seedpod look like the samples you have collected, and wrap it tightly with damp paper towels and plastic so that it will dry slowly. Check it frequently to detect any cracking where parts have been joined. Repair these cracks with slip and your modeling tool.

Modeling Flower Buds

Following the instructions for making a seed head, model flower buds as decorative elements. They should be hollow, because solid lumps of clay may crack while drying and firing, but their walls can be as thick as ½ inch (13 mm) for ease of handling and for strength. Make one or two unopened buds. The stems for these should be more slender than those for the leaves; plan on using ¼-inch (6 mm) tubing, and size the collars to fit.

An unopened flower bud (top), a spouting seed head (middle), and a partially opened bud (bottom).

Fire and Finish the Clay Pieces

Allow all pieces to dry slowly and thoroughly. When you have felt no dampness or coolness in the clay for at least a week, take them to the kiln and have them fired. As with any large clay piece, the larger leaves will require especially long warm-up and cool-down periods. If you find any small stress cracks in the clay after firing, fill these with epoxy.

Portable *Tsukubai* Fountain

This adaptation of the Japanese *Tsukubai* is a small, portable fountain suitable for use indoors and out, in even the smallest of spaces. The spout for this fountain is soldered from copper tubing to resemble bamboo. Wire is soldered around the tubing at intervals to suggest joints, and wrapped where the two pieces intersect to bind them together, as you would bamboo. You can substitute a spout of real bamboo, such as that featured in the Concrete Coin Basin project (page 119), if you don't have metalworking equipment available to you.

◄ By using a reservoir with a flattened side, you can create a wall-hung fountain.

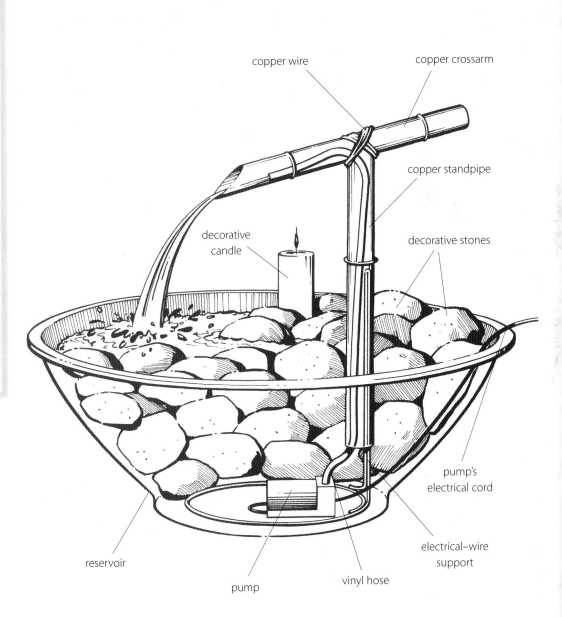

copper wire

copper crossarm

copper standpipe

decorative candle

decorative stones

pump's electrical cord

electrical–wire support

vinyl hose

pump

reservoir

For the Reservoir
• Large bowl of ceramic, metal, or resin

For the Pump
• Pump, 80 GPH (304 l per hour)
• GFCI outlet

Fountain Elements
• Rigid copper tubing for "bamboo" spout: 1 8" (20 cm) piece of 1" (2.5 cm) diameter; 1 9" (22.5 cm) piece of ³/₄" (19 mm) diameter
• 18-gauge copper wire

• Patina solution (for homemade recipe, see Antiquing Cooper on page 114)
• ¹/₄" (6 mm) ID vinyl hose: 2' (60 cm), plus short pieces of larger diameters if needed to fit pump
• 3' (1 m) stiff electrical wire such as Romex, about 14 gauge, insulation and all (for wire spout support)
• 5–10 pounds (2.3–4.5 kg) small river stones of varying sizes, a few as large as small baking potatoes

Tools
• Silicone caulk (optional)
• Hacksaw

• Files, flat and round
• Drill press or variable-speed hand drill
• Center punch
• Clamps or vise
• ¹/₂" (13 mm) drill bit for metal (twist bit)
• Steel wool or scouring pad
• Soldering flux with brush
• Disposable gas torch
• Solder
• Pliers, wire nippers
• Cotton swabs

Selecting the Reservoir

You'll need to find an attractive bowl for the reservoir. The bowl you select should be at least 4 inches (10 cm) deep and 16 inches (40 cm) in diameter. Any material that holds water will serve the purpose: ceramic, metal, polyester resin. If the material tends to sweat, as terra-cotta often does, you can stop this by coating the inside of the bowl with silicone caulk. Allow this to dry thoroughly.

A slightly damp reservoir will also work well on a stand made of metal; these are often sold in good garden centers. Usually made of wrought iron, they support the reservoir several inches off the table and thus protect surfaces from pots that sweat slightly.

tip If you wish to substitute real bamboo for copper in this project, you can. Follow step 3 in the *Shishi Odoshi* project (page 59), but reduce the height of the spout to about 6 inches (15 cm), so that it won't splash. Cut the extra length from the bottom of the faucet standpipe. Of course, any other changes in proportion required for your particular reservoir can be made freely.

◀ Fill the reservoir with a variety of polished stones; the flowing water will accentuate their natural beauty.

Constructing the Spout

▶ Step 1: Cut the Spout Parts

For the standpipe, cut an 8-inch (20 cm) length of 1-inch (2.5 cm) ID copper tubing with a hacksaw. Cut one end square and the other at a slight angle — about 15 degrees. With a file or grinder, create a slight cradle in the high and low sides of this cut to hold the crossarm securely. Now cut a 9-inch (22.5 cm) crossarm from ¾-inch (19 mm) ID tubing. Cut one end square and the other, from which the water will flow, at a sharp angle — about 30 degrees. Smooth all cuts with your file. ▼

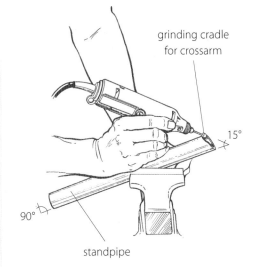

grinding cradle for crossarm

15°

90°

standpipe

▶ Step 2: Drill the Crossarm

Now you need to drill a hole for the vinyl hose in the crossarm, ½ inch (13 mm) in diameter. This is best done on a drill press, but if you don't have one, try the following: With a nail or center punch, make a dent in the bottom of the crossarm approximately 5 inches (12.5 cm) from the pointed end, on the same side of the tube as the long end of the point. (This will be the bottom side of the crossarm.) Clamp the tubing securely to your bench to do this. Then, using a ½-inch (13 mm) drill bit at slow speed, drill through the tubing where you made the dent. Remember to use slow speed and a few drops of oil to lubricate the drill as it breaks through the wall of the tubing. ▼

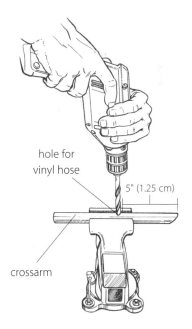

hole for vinyl hose

5" (1.25 cm)

crossarm

▶ Step 3: Solder the Spout

Thoroughly clean the tubing with steel wool or a scouring pad. Set the crossarm on the standpipe and be sure you understand how they should fit together. The pointed end of the crossarm should be lower than the square end. The ½-inch (13 mm) hole should be oriented directly above the top of the standpipe. Now flip the whole assembly upside down and prepare to solder it together. It needs to be supported on a fireproof surface such as bricks, and propped up in an upside-down orientation.

Brush flux onto the two places where the standpipe touches the crossarm — both in front of and behind the ½-inch (13 mm) hole. Then light a gas torch and, using solder wire, spot-solder the two pieces together. ▼

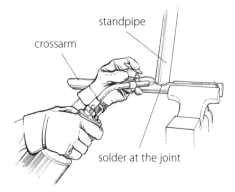

standpipe

crossarm

solder at the joint

▶ Step 4: Wrap the Spout

Next, wrap 18-gauge copper wire neatly around the connection in a figure-eight pattern. Twist the ends together at the back, clipping them off with about two twists projecting; you'll trim them flush later. Now wrap a double wrap of wire around the standpipe and crossarm every 4 to 6 inches (10 to 15 cm) to suggest the joints in bamboo. Twist the ends together and clip them off, leaving two twists. Brush flux on all wire wraps. ▼

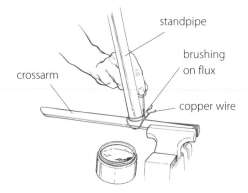

standpipe

brushing on flux

crossarm

copper wire

Heat each wire wrap and twisted end until solder runs beneath the wires, bonding them to the tubing. Then nip the twists off neatly close to the tubing — the wire shouldn't unwrap. Smooth any rough spots with your file. ▼

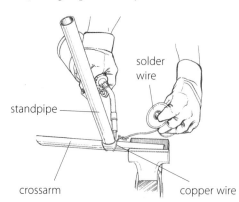

solder wire

standpipe

crossarm

copper wire

Three Soldering Tips

1. Adjust the flame of the gas torch until the blue center cone is an inch (2.5 cm) or so long. This blue cone is the "hot spot," the part of the flame that actually does the work of soldering.

2. Hold the solder wire up to the spot to be soldered and focus the tip of the flame's blue center cone on that spot until the tip of the solder wire melts as it touches the metal and runs, by capillary action, between the pieces to be joined. It helps to have the assembly upside down so that gravity will help place the solder where you want it to go.

3. Wear protective glasses, clothing, and gloves while soldering: Hot solder may splatter and burn your skin.

▶ Step 5: Finish the Spout with Patina

Before you apply patina, thoroughly clean all grease or flux from the copper. You can do this in hot water with a good soap-filled scouring pad. Scrub until you have thoroughly etched the surface with a maze of tiny scratches and no trace of grease remains. Then, using a cotton swab, soak the surface with the patina solution.

Putting It All Together

▶ Step 1: Insert the Hose into the Spout

Now it's time to insert a 24-inch (60 cm) length of ¼-inch (6 mm) ID clear vinyl hose into your spout. If you have a vise, put a ½-inch (13 mm) dowel or other similar stick in it so that it stands upright (a wooden spoon clamped horizontally to a table would also work). Thread the hose into the standpipe and wiggle it so that it passes through the ½-inch (13 mm) hole into the crossarm. Now slide the upper (back) end of the crossarm over the dowel, so that the dowel bumps against the hose where it projects into the crossarm. Feeding more hose into the bottom of the standpipe, repeatedly bump the hose onto the dowel to force the hose to make the tight turn toward the front of the crossarm. Keep this up until the hose has progressed a few inches past the turn.

▶ Step 2: Make a Wire Support for the Spout

Form a piece of stiff electrical wire about 3 feet (1 m) long — Romex, which is used to wire the walls in houses, works well, insulation and all — into a round hoop 8 inches (20 cm) across, which will sit on the bottom of your bowl. Where the hoop closes, bend the remaining wire up at 90 degrees for a 4- to 5-inch (10 to 12.5 cm) support post. This can be folded back down on itself for more strength. Flatten this fold so that you can fit the support post into the copper tube with the hose. Trim off any extra length or bend it to follow the hoop. ▼

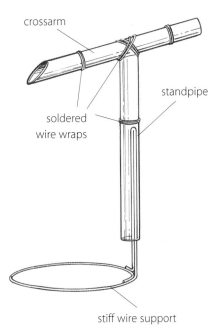

crossarm

soldered wire wraps

standpipe

stiff wire support

▶ Step 3: Install the Fountain

In a waterproof work area, place the pump in the bowl and fill the bowl with water. The hose, which should not be readily visible from the spout end, should project from the bottom of the standpipe only about an inch (2.5 cm). Make sure the hose in the spout will fit the pump's outflow. If the ¼-inch (6 mm) ID hose that's inserted in the spout does not fit the pump, telescope lengths of successively larger sizes until it fits. Then plug in the pump.

Push the spout onto the wire support post, adjust the pump's flow control to low, and fit the spout's vinyl tubing onto the pump. Pile the river stones over the wire support and pump. The pump's cord should be led over the edge of the bowl, concealed by stones.

By leaving a pool of water beneath the tip of the spout, you can create a small sounding chamber where the peaceful trickle of water from the spout can be amplified throughout the room. Take care to keep the fountain from splashing. The flow should be very gentle and peaceful. You can adjust the arrangement of the stones if necessary to prevent droplets from jumping over the edge of the bowl.

Birdshower Fountain

Derived from the *Tsukubai,* this fountain provides your garden with a spacious birdbath constantly watered by a "bamboo" spout of soldered copper. The sound of falling water is very attractive to birds, which will use the fountain for drinking as well as for bathing. The reservoir can be hidden beneath the birdbath so that the pond is inaccessible, making this fountain a good choice for a location where small children or playful dogs are present.

You will need to be able to solder the copper tube; this requires a small gas torch and a fireproof surface upon which to work. If you prefer, you may instead substitute the bamboo spout described in the Concrete Coin Basin project (page 119). In addition, the sandcasting process requires some use of a table saw to make the mold parts.

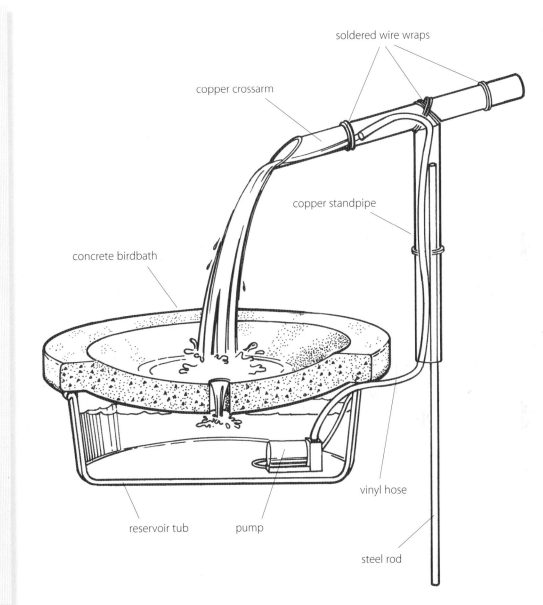

soldered wire wraps

copper crossarm

copper standpipe

concrete birdbath

vinyl hose

reservoir tub

pump

steel rod

For the Reservoir
- 1 concrete birdbath with drainage hole (see Sandcasting a Concrete Birdbath on pages 116–117)
- 16" (40 cm) diameter bucket or tub

For the Pump
- Pump with variable flow control, 140 GPH (532 l per hour)
- GFCI outlet or GFCI extension cord

Fountain Elements
- $1/2$" (13 mm) ID vinyl tubing: 6" (15 cm)
- Rigid copper tubing for "bamboo" spout: 1 18" (45 cm) piece of 1" (2.5 cm) diameter; 1 12" (30 cm) piece of $3/4$" (19 mm) diameter
- 18-gauge copper wire: approximately 5' (1.5 m)
- Patina mixture, commercial or homemade
- $1/4$" (6 mm) ID vinyl hose: 3' (1 m), plus short lengths of larger sizes as needed
- 24" (60 cm) length of re-bar, or any steel rod

Tools
- Hacksaw
- Files, flat and round
- Drill press or variable-speed hand drill
- Center punch
- Clamps or vise
- $1/2$" (13 mm) drill bit for metal (twist bit)
- Steel wool or scouring pad
- Soldering flux with brush
- Disposable gas torch
- Solder
- Pliers, wire nippers
- Cotton swabs
- Plastic cup

This alternative "birdshower" version of the *tsukubai* fountain has a large, cubed reservoir — not the sort that you'd make at home, but you might be able to find one for purchase.

Constructing the Spout

▶ Step 1: Cut the Spout Parts

The spout for this fountain is soldered from copper plumbing tubing to resemble bamboo. Wire is soldered around the tubing at intervals to suggest the joints, and wrapped where the two pieces intersect to bind them together as you would bamboo.

For the standpipe, cut an 18-inch (45 cm) length of 1-inch (2.5 cm) ID copper tubing with a hacksaw. Cut one end square and the other at a slight angle — about 15 degrees. With a file, create a slight cradle in the high and low sides of this angled cut to hold the crossarm securely. Now cut a 12-inch (30 cm) crossarm from ¾-inch (19 mm) ID tubing. Cut one end square and the other end, from which the water will flow, at a sharp angle — about 30 degrees. Smooth all cuts with your file. ▼

▶ Step 2: Drill through the Crossarm

Now you need to drill a hole in the crossarm, ½ inch (13 mm) in diameter. This is best done on a drill press, but if you don't have one, try the following: With a nail or center punch, make a dent in the bottom of the crossarm approximately 8 inches (20 cm) from the pointed end, on the same side of the tubing as the long end of the point. (This will be the bottom side of the crossarm.) Clamp the tubing securely to your bench to do this. Then, using a ½-inch (13 mm) drill bit at slow speed, drill through the tubing where you made the dent. Remember to use slow speed and a few drops of oil to lubricate the drill as it breaks through the wall of the tubing. ▼

▶ Step 3: Solder the Spout Parts

Thoroughly clean the tubing with steel wool or a scouring pad. Then set the crossarm on the standpipe and be sure you understand how they should fit together. The pointed end of the crossarm should be lower than the square end. The ½-inch (13 mm) hole should be oriented above the top of the standpipe. When you're ready, flip the whole assembly upside down and prepare to solder it together. It needs to be supported on a fireproof surface, such as bricks, or clamped securely to a table, and propped up in an upside-down orientation.

If you're unfamiliar with the technique of soldering, review Three Soldering Tips on page 108. Then brush flux onto the two places where the standpipe touches the crossarm — both in front of and behind the ½-inch (13 mm) hole. Light a gas torch and, using solder wire, spot-solder the two pieces together. ▼

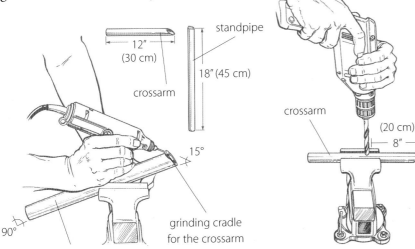

standpipe
12" (30 cm)
crossarm
18" (45 cm)
15°
grinding cradle for the crossarm
90°
standpipe

crossarm
(20 cm)
8"

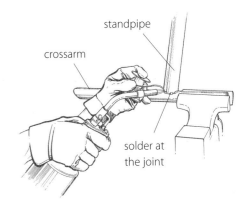

standpipe
crossarm
solder at the joint

▶ Step 4: Wrap the Spout

Wrap 18-gauge copper wire neatly around the connection in a figure-eight pattern. Twist the ends of the wire together at the back to fasten them, clipping them off with about two twists projecting; you'll trim them flush later. Wrap a double wrap of wire around the standpipe and crossarm every 4 to 6 inches (10 to 15 cm) to suggest the joints in bamboo, twist the ends together, and clip them off, leaving two twists. Brush flux onto each of the wire wraps. ▼

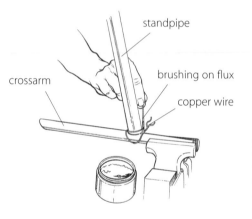

standpipe

crossarm

brushing on flux

copper wire

Holding the solder at the twist, heat each wire wrap until solder runs beneath the wires, bonding them to the tubing. Then you can nip the twists off neatly close to the tubing without the wire unwrapping. Smooth any rough spots with your file. ▼

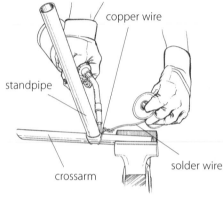

copper wire

standpipe

crossarm

solder wire

▶ Step 5: Finish the Spout with Patina

Before you apply patina, thoroughly clean all grease or flux from the copper spout. You can do this in hot water with a good soap-filled scouring pad. Scrub until you have thoroughly etched the surface with a maze of tiny scratches and no trace of grease remains. Then, using a cotton swab or a spray bottle, soak the surface of the copper parts with the commercial patina solution or one made according to the instructions in Antiquing Copper (see below).

Antiquing Copper

In nature, copper oxidizes to a blue-green patina. If you want your copper to look old but don't want to wait out the several months of weathering necessary for it to happen naturally, you can coat it with a solution to make it oxidize quickly. Craft supply stores sell patina solutions. You can also make one yourself from salt and muriatic acid, which is sold in hardware stores for cleaning brick.

1. Dissolve 1 part table salt in 1 part warm water. Allow this to cool, then place in a plastic cup.
2. Add 3 parts muriatic acid.
3. Apply with a cotton swab and let dry to obtain the full effect.
4. Recoat the copper until you obtain your desired color.

Handle this caustic solution with care, wear eye protection, and dispose of any unused solution by pouring it down the sink or storing it in a clearly labeled acidproof bottle.

Putting It All Together

▶ Step 1: Insert the Hose into the Spout

Now it's time to insert a 24-inch (60 cm) length of ¼-inch (6 mm) ID clear vinyl hose into your spout. If you have a vise, put a ½-inch (13 mm) dowel or other similar stick in it so that it stands upright (a wooden spoon clamped horizontally to a table would also work). Thread the hose into the standpipe and wiggle it so that it passes through the ½-inch (13 mm) hole into the crossarm. Now slide the upper (back) end of the crossarm over the dowel, so that the dowel bumps against the hose where it projects into the crossarm. Feeding more hose into the bottom of the standpipe, repeatedly bump the hose onto the dowel to force the hose to make the tight turn toward the front of the crossarm. Keep this up until the hose has progressed a few inches past the turn.

▶ Step 2: Bury the Reservoir

Select a plastic tub or bucket for your reservoir. For an 18-inch (45 cm) birdbath, a tub diameter of 16 inches (40 cm) is ideal. The diameter of the reservoir must be smaller than that of the birdbath, so that the bath serves as a lid for the reservoir, keeping dirt and debris from falling into it. At the same time, the shower works best if the diameter of the reservoir is large enough for the bath to sit low inside it so as to contain a shallow pool of water. Cut a notch in the rim of the reservoir large enough to accommodate both the vinyl hose from the spout and the electric cord from the pump. Dig a hole large enough to hold the reservoir. Place it in the hole and set the pump inside.

▶ Step 3: Connect the Spout to the Reservoir

Drive the length of re-bar vertically into the ground. Drop the standpipe of the "bamboo" spout over it and plug the vinyl hose into the pump. You may need to telescope short sections of larger sizes to adapt to the size of the pump's outflow. Fill the reservoir with water and plug in the pump. Adjust the flow control until the pump works the way you want it to. Place the birdbath over the reservoir. A shallow pool of water should remain in the bath when the reservoir is full.

▶ Step 4: Add Final Touches

Now you can landscape around the fountain with stones and plantings. The Birdshower Fountain will require refilling at intervals, depending on heat and humidity, but you should be able to do this without dismantling the bath by running your garden hose into the birdbath.

> **tip** If you live in colder regions and will drain and store the fountain and reservoir through the freezing months, clean the pump thoroughly before storing so that algae will not dry inside it.

Tsukubai fountains come in many shapes and forms. This "birdshower" version uses a squared-off reservoir with a basin molded into its center.

Sandcasting a Concrete Birdbath

The instructions that follow detail how to cast a beautifully textured concrete birdbath. The dimensions given will result in a bath suitable for use in the Birdshower Fountain (beginning on page 111). However, you could use this bath as a wonderful feature anywhere in your yard or garden. Simply omit the drainage hole described, set the finished concrete piece on a picturesque pedestal, and let the birds enjoy!

Make a Template

Find a piece of plastic laminate or ⅛-inch (3 mm) Masonite about a foot (30 cm) square. On it, draw one half of the birdbath full sized in cross section, upside down. The baseline should be 9 inches (22.5 cm) wide, representing half the 18-inch (45 cm) diameter, from the center of the drain hole to the outside edge. Draw another line ½ inch (13 mm) above the baseline, to represent the surface of the sand layer at the rim, where the sand is only ½ inch deep. On the centerline mark a point 5½ inches (14 cm) above the baseline, to represent the depth of the sand layer in the center of the bowl — 5 inches (12.5 cm) above the rim in this inverted picture.

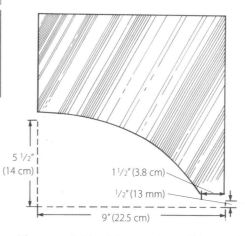

5 ½″ (14 cm) 1 ½″ (3.8 cm) ½″ (13 mm) 9″ (22.5 cm)

The curved side of the template will be used to shape the sand mold.

Draw a gently rounded curve from the deepest point of the bowl (5½ inches, or 14 cm, up the centerline) to the inside of the flat rim (1½ inches, or 3.8 cm, inside the outside edge), representing the top surface of the sand. Cut out the shape with the curved side for use as a template in shaping the sand mold.

Construct the Sand Mold

On a 24-inch (60 cm) square of plywood, draw a circle with an 18-inch (45 cm) diameter. Using a table saw so that the cuts will be square, cut a strip of plastic laminate 6 inches (15 cm) wide by 57 inches (145 cm) long. With a black marker, draw a line down one long edge of this strip, 1 inch (2.5 cm) from the edge. Draw a second line 2 inches (5 cm) from the edge. These will remain visible above the sand and concrete

levels, giving you a guide to their thickness as you smooth them into shape.

Wrap this flexible strip into a circular collar until the ends butt together. Hold it in this position by spring-clamping both sides of the joint to a short scrap of same-width material. Arrange this collar on the circle you have drawn and adjust it until it closely follows the shape. You may need to move the spring clamps closer together or farther apart to make the butt joint smoothly follow the curve of the circle. Tape the entire outside of the joint between the collar and the plywood with duct tape. If you're using Masonite, grease its inside with petroleum jelly.

Mix a bucketful of sand with enough water to almost saturate it. This will make a mixture that packs tightly and is hard to disturb. Pour a pile of this sand mix into the center of the mold and form it with your hands into a soft,

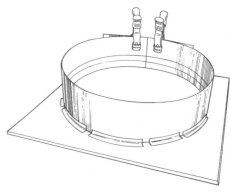

Clamp together the two ends of the plastic laminate to create the circular collar that will contain the sand mold.

curving hump about 5 inches (12.5 cm) high. Leave a 1½-inch (3.8 cm) wide groove around the edge where the sand is only ½ inch (13 mm) deep, to form the rim of the birdbath. Using the template you have cut from the layout, gently scrape the surface of the sand mold until it has a uniform and smooth shape. Excess sand must be removed from the mold. Pat and smooth with your hands any tears and scrapes in the sand surface.

The drain in the bottom of the birdbath is formed by casting a piece of tubing into the concrete. Slide a length of ½-inch (13 mm) ID hose onto a ½-inch dowel about 12 inches (30 cm) long, grease the hose well with petroleum jelly, and push the dowel vertically into the center of the mold. Slide the hose down until it just penetrates the sand. This dowel must remain undisturbed while you pour the concrete.

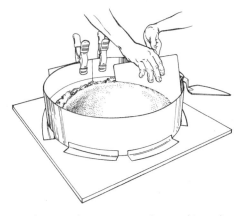

Use the template to scrape the sand into the proper form. Remove any excess sand.

Pour the Concrete

Mix a 25-pound (11.4 kg) bag of premixed concrete according to the directions on the bag (see also Working with Concrete on page 87). The best place to mix it is a wheelbarrow or plastic dishpan — wide, shallow containers make it easier for you to get at the clumps of dry concrete. The mix should look thoroughly wet but not shiny — there should be no extra water. If you feel that it's too wet, sprinkle another trowelful of concrete mix over it and mix this in. (Adding thin layers of dry powder after the mix is smooth is a good way to arrive at the right point.) The important thing is strong concrete, made without excessive water.

Beginning at the bottom, drop the mix into the outer lip groove of the mold in a layer about 1 inch (2.5 cm) thick. By gently chopping into it, distribute it evenly around the edge of the mold. Smooth it with the trowel to press out the air. Moving up the sand pile, add concrete in a blanket about 1½ inches (3.8 cm) thick. Superficially making small chopping and spreading motions, pack it tightly with the trowel. If you feel that you haven't mixed enough concrete, use what you have in a complete thin coat so that the color will be consistent over the entire inside surface. Then add a second batch to build up the thickness. Aim for 1 to 1½ inches (2.5 to 3.8 cm) in thickness overall. Keep smoothing the concrete with

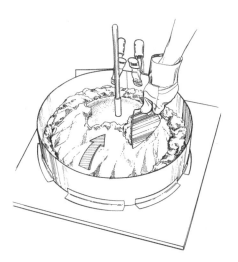

Gently chop and spread the concrete to form a thick blanket over the sand mold.

the trowel to squeeze out air, which makes it stronger. When finished, cover the setting concrete with a damp towel to allow slow drying, and set aside for 24 hours.

Remove the Concrete Casting

After 24 hours, open the mold by removing the sides and lift the concrete gently from the sand. Hose it down and scrub it with a wire brush to remove excess sand and enhance the surface texture. Remember that concrete is soft and weak when first cast, so you can most easily scrape off any unwanted globs at this point. Drive the dowel and hose from the concrete with gentle taps from a hammer.

Then replace the wet towel and wrap the concrete casting with plastic. It needs three days to fully cure. After this point, you may handle it less carefully.

Concrete Coin Basin with Bamboo Spout

The simple yet elegant coin fountain is famous in the Zen tradition and features a stone carved in the shape of a Japanese coin: a short round cylinder with a square recess in the center. Some are very detailed, including Japanese characters. Some are more primitive with very rough surfaces.

The reservoir of this outdoor fountain is buried in the ground, making this design suitable for soft-soil areas of the garden rather than paved terraces. Still, it's nice to locate it close to a bench or terraced area, so that you can sit nearby and appreciate the subtlety of its shape and sound. You can make the coin fountain in any size you can handle. The version here is relatively small, with a basin only 12 inches (30 cm) in diameter. The concrete takes some time to cure, so this project will take you a few days to complete.

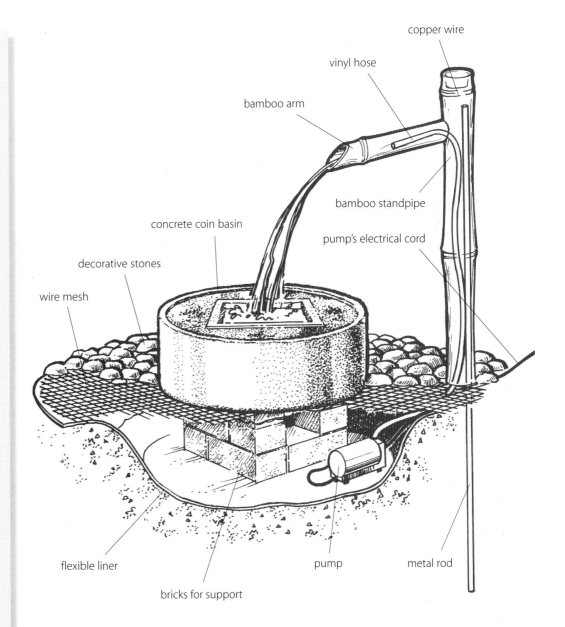

copper wire

vinyl hose

bamboo arm

bamboo standpipe

concrete coin basin

pump's electrical cord

decorative stones

wire mesh

flexible liner

pump

metal rod

bricks for support

MATERIALS

For the Reservoir
- Tub or flexible liner for underground reservoir, 24" (60 cm) square minimum (can substitute heavy black plastic)
- 1/4" (6 mm) galvanized wire mesh: piece to cover reservoir

For the Pump
- Pump, 140 GPH (532 l per hour)
- GFCI outlet

Fountain Elements
- 25 pounds (11.4 kg) premixed concrete mix or ingredients (see Working with Concrete on page 87)
- Bamboo: several feet (about 1 m) each of 2" and 3/4" (5 and 1.9 cm) diameters

- 1/4" (6 mm) ID vinyl hose: 3' (90 cm)
- Natural twine or copper wire
- 8–12 bricks
- 2–3' (60–90 cm) length of concrete rebar or other metal rod

Decorative Elements
- 50 pounds (22.7 kg) small beach stones

Tools
- 5–10 pounds (2.3–4.5 kg) builder's sand
- Plastic bucket, such as the kind used for drywall compound — sides flared as little as possible
- Plastic food container, 4" (10 cm) square x 4" high (as a form for the sand mold; can substitute a round container)
- Whittling knife

- Block of wood
- Spray bottle
- Popsicle stick or chopstick
- Wire brush
- Paper towels
- Sheet of lightweight plastic, such as the kind dry cleaning is wrapped in
- Sharp saw
- Electric drill with Forstner bit, about 3/4" (19 mm)
- Clamps or vise
- Sandpaper

This larger version of the coin basin fountain is set up on a stone platform, lending it a sense of stature and permanence in the garden.

Casting the Coin Basin

▶ Step 1: Prepare the Sand Mold

Mix 2 quarts (1.9 l) of sand with enough water to almost completely saturate it. Pour a 1-inch (2.5 cm) deep layer of this into the bucket and smooth it so that it forms a level surface. Then pack more of this mixture into a plastic container 4 inches (10 cm) square by 4 inches high. Carefully invert this in the center of the sand floor in the bucket and tap it to loosen and free the plastic container. You should have a square block of sand centered in the bucket.

If the sides of the block seem less straight than you want them, carve the sand with a knife to make the sides straight. Now tamp the sand on the floor of the bucket with the end of a block of wood to pack it firm. If the sand dries as you work, mist it occasionally with a spray bottle of water.

The last step is to groove the sand around the square block and around the outside of the floor to create the impression of a coin with thickened edges. Use a popsicle stick or chopstick. Remove any displaced sand. ▼

▶ Step 2: Cast the Concrete Basin

Mix the cement with the sand, unless you're using premixed concrete. Carefully stir the water into the dry mixture. Remember, too much water will weaken the final product; too little will result in a finished piece full of air bubbles. Try to keep the concrete mix as dry as possible, while taking care to wet all of it evenly. You should be able to see a shine on the surface if you smooth it with a trowel, but it should be a stiff mix. (See Working with Concrete on page 87 for tips and techniques.)

Gently scoop the cement into the mold in handfuls and tamp it with the flat end of a dowel or strip of wood until it is about 9 inches (22.5 cm) deep. Let it set for 48 hours, then cut the drywall bucket with a knife to remove it from the concrete. Rinse the sand free from the concrete with water to reveal the surface. Roughen any surfaces that look too smooth with a wire brush. Cover the coin basin with damp paper towels and plastic for a three-day curing period.

Building the Spout

▶ Step 1: Cut the Spout Parts

Before you begin, review Working with Bamboo on page 41. You will need to cut two bamboo pieces for the spout:

- A vertical piece, or standpipe, measuring about 2 inches (5 cm) in diameter and 20 inches (50 cm) high
- A short horizontal chute, or arm, measuring about ¾-inch (19 mm) in diameter and 6 inches (15 cm) long.

These dimensions are a starting point. You may find an attractive combination in other sizes that works well for your fountain. Cut the bamboo with square ends except for the outer end of the arm, which should be cut at a sharp angle (about 30 degrees). Sand the cut ends but keep the angled cut as clean and flat as possible, without rounding the edges.

plastic bucket

square block of sand

grooves in sand

1" (2.5 cm) layer of sand

Cutting Bamboo

When cutting the standpipe piece, notice the location of the natural walls in the bamboo. You will have to drill out any wall that occurs where hose must pass inside the bamboo. Rather than avoid these beautiful features, see to it that they are located where drilling will be easy or unnecessary. Arrange the cuts so that one wall occurs just inside the top of the standpipe. This forms a natural cap and will not need to be drilled. Another wall will probably occur down low on the standpipe. This should be drilled out, but if it's close to the end of the piece you can do so with a simple drill bit.

Step 2: Fit the Arm in the Standpipe

Clamp the standpipe in a vise or to a bench and drill a hole sized for the horizontal arm about 2 inches (5 cm) from its top. This is easiest to do with a Forstner bit the same size as the arm. Insert the arm stock into the hole in the standpipe to make sure you have a tight fit, then trim the arm to length. Remove the arm.

Step 3: Insert the Hose

Now thread a 3-foot (1 m) piece of ¼-inch (6 mm) ID vinyl hose through the standpipe and allow it to hang loose from the armhole. Slide the arm over the hose and push it tightly into its hole. Pull the hose back until you can't see it protruding from the arm. ▼

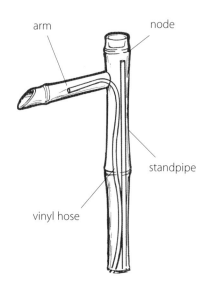

arm   node

standpipe

vinyl hose

Step 4: Wrap the Spout

When used as a fountain piece, where its outside dries and its inside is kept wet, bamboo is bound to split. The uneven moisture causes swelling inside and shrinking outside, building up pressure that is relieved by the formation of a crack. The best approach to this is to expect it and use it as an opportunity for further decoration. Wrap the bamboo pieces that form the spout at several points, especially near the slanted end of the horizontal arm, with natural twine or copper wire. Wrap the wire around two or three times. Twist the ends tightly together and snip off, leaving at least two twists so that the wire won't unravel.

Forming the Underground Reservoir

Step 1: Dig the Hole

Dig a hole for the underground reservoir. Make it at least 8 inches (20 cm) bigger in diameter than the coin basin and able to hold at least 5 gallons (19 l) of water, or about 6 to 8 inches (15 to 20 cm) deep and 24 to 30 inches (60 to 75 cm) wide. Make the bottom level for even support of the coin basin. Try stacking the support bricks inside at this point to be sure their top surface is slightly lower than the edge of the reservoir. Smooth the soil in the hole so that no sharp roots or stones will project to pierce the liner once it's stretched full of water.

Step 2: Line the Hole

Spread the pond liner or heavy black plastic into the hole. If you're using plastic sheets, use many layers, in case one has a small hole in it. Set the bricks permanently into the reservoir now, and on them support a piece of ¼-inch (6 mm) galvanized mesh large enough to cover the pool. On top of this set the coin basin.

Choosing the Right Material

EPDM, a rubber compound, is generally agreed to be the best and longest-lasting pond liner. You can buy it from many home supply, garden supply, and pond supply stores. It is somewhat expensive, however. For a small and temporary installation such as this one, you may substitute several layers of heavy black plastic such as that used to wrap lumber deliveries or to make good-quality trash bags. After all, the reservoir will be hidden from view, and in many climates, it will be disassembled and drained for the winter. In addition, if it develops a leak, the consequences of having to replace its liner are very small.

Setting Up the Fountain

▶ Step 1: Erect the Spout Support

Make a support for the spout by driving a piece of re-bar or other metal rod into the soil. Slide the standpipe over the rod and your spout will be supported.

▶ Step 2: Set Up the Pump

Remove the coin basin and make a small cut in the wire mesh. Set the pump into the reservoir, fill it with water, and pass the hose from the spout through the cut in the wire mesh to plug it into the pump. Replace the coin basin. If necessary, pull your fountain apart and lower the support for the basin so that the mesh sags into the center, leading all water back to the reservoir. ▼

▶ Step 3: Test the Water Flow

At this point you should plug the pump into a GFCI outlet and test the system. The water should fall in a gentle arc from the spout into the square well in the center of the coin fountain. Filling this well, the water should overflow into the underground reservoir to be pumped back to the spout.

▶ Step 4: Add Finishing Touches

When you are satisfied with the relationships of the parts, trim the liner to size. Spread small beach stones or large pea gravel over the mesh and around the coin basin and spout. The rough sandcast surface of the basin should make it look like an ancient artifact. In time moss may grow on it in the humid environment of the fountain. You can plant clumps of moss and ferns among the beach stones for the effect of an established Zen garden. You can also make a small bamboo dipper (see Bamboo Dipper on page 43) and place it across the pool in the coin basin.

ⓑ tip If the fountain begins to run low, adding water is easy: Simply use your garden hose to pour water directly onto the coin basin and beach stones.

hole cut in mesh for vinyl hose and electrical cord

flexible liner

bricks for support

pump

metal rod

If you can find one of the Japanese coins that serve as a model for the fountain base, copy the symbols on its surface onto the base.

Cast-Stone Sluice Flowing into Hypertufa Trough

This outdoor fountain requires a site where you have or can build a low stone retaining wall at the edge of a level terrace. This retaining wall in turn surrounds a concrete sluice from which water pours into a trough made of hypertufa — stone you can cast yourself. The simplicity of the design is very appealing, tricking the observer into the belief that this is a naturally occurring spring flowing from a rustic spillway installed by earlier hands.

The rustic trough is formed from hypertufa cast around a Styrofoam box, resulting in a relatively lightweight reservoir. The concrete sluice is made from a sandcasting mold. The curing times for both of these materials makes this a long-term project, one that you will have to set aside for days or weeks at a time before moving on to the next step.

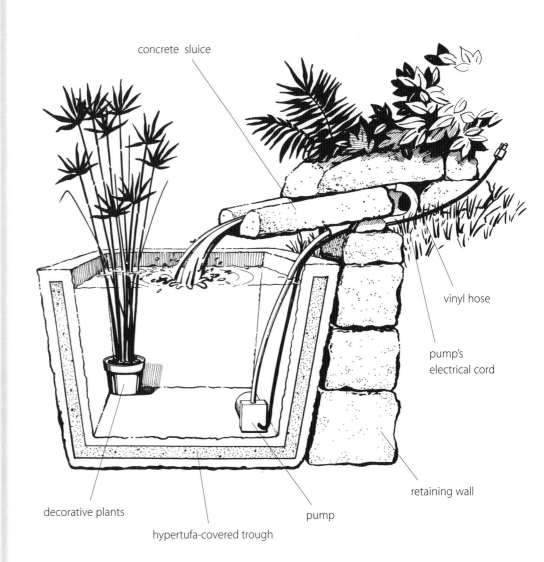

concrete sluice

vinyl hose

pump's electrical cord

retaining wall

decorative plants

pump

hypertufa-covered trough

MATERIALS

Fountain and Reservoir Elements
- Plywood sheet; approximately $2^1/_2$" x 12" (6.3 x 30 cm), to form outside dimensions of sluice
- About 7' (2 m) of 1 x 3 lumber to frame plywood
- 15 pounds (6.8 kg) Portland cement (a mix of white and gray if available)
- 5 pounds (2.3 kg) sphagnum peat moss, sifted to remove sticks and chunks
- Styrofoam box, at least 12 x 16 x 8" (30 x 40 x 20 cm)
- 3–4' (1–1.2 m) vinyl hose, sized to fit pump's outflow; plus 2–3' (0.6–1 m) garden or vinyl hose sized large enough to fit loosely over this

For the Pump
- Pump, 140 GPH (532 l per hour)
- GFCI outlet

Tools
- Drywall screws, for mold assembly
- 30 pounds (13.6 kg) sharp mason's sand
- Plastic tub or wheelbarrow
- Flat mason's trowel
- Wire brush
- Paper towels
- Sheet of lightweight plastic, such as the kind dry cleaning is wrapped in
- 1-quart (1 l) yogurt container
- Yellow wood glue and brush
- Wide mixing tub

Depending on the size of your trough, you can plant a variety of water plants. Some of the best ones to consider are water lilies (shown here), water hyacinth, dwarf papyrus, iris, and cattails.

Hypertufa History

Hypertufa is a material developed by English alpine gardeners. Because alpine plants thrive when grown in porous stone troughs, and because the supply of old stone livestock troughs has dried up, these inventive folks have developed a mixture of peat, sand, and cement that, when fully cured, looks and behaves like the limestone they are seeking to replace.

Casting the Concrete Sluice

▶ Step 1: Construct the Plywood Frame

First, construct a shallow box of plywood and 1 x 3 wood strips. The inside should measure approximately 2½ inches (6.3 cm) wide by 12 inches (30 cm) long. Screw the sides to the bottom for easy removal. The corners, since they will be filled with sand, do not have to be especially tight. Simply allow the sides to overlap the ends and fasten with one screw per corner.

▶ Step 2: Mold the Sand

Mix 2 quarts (2l) of sand with enough water to nearly saturate it, so that it packs tightly and is hard to disturb. Drop a pile of this mix into the center of the mold and spread it over the bottom. Form it with your hands into a soft, curving hump down the center, about 1 inch (2.5 cm) high and wide. Leave a ¾-inch (19 mm) wide groove down both long sides where the sand is only ¼ inch (6 mm) deep, to form the raised edges of the sluice.

Pile extra sand into all the corners and seams of the box and run your finger along them to produce a rounded edge in the concrete. Make this somewhat more exaggerated in the short end from which water will ultimately pour from the completed sluice, so as to form a rounded lip for the spillway. ▼

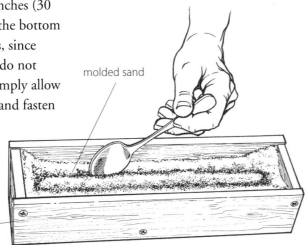

molded sand

plywood frame

▶ Step 3: Pour the Concrete

Mix 1 quart (1 l) of Portland cement with 2½ quarts (2½ l) of fresh mason's sand. Use a proportion of 2 parts cement to 5 parts sand. When this is thoroughly mixed, add just enough water to thoroughly dampen all the dry powder and mix this thoroughly. Add water very sparingly; the concrete will be far stronger if mixed quite dry. When you smooth the surface with the trowel, it should have a wet shine.

Drop the concrete gently into the mold with the trowel and tamp it as you go with the flat end of a dowel or handle of the trowel, taking care not to disturb the sand mold below. Mound it up in the mold so as to follow the inside shape and produce a sluice of an even thickness — about 1½ inches (3.8 cm).

ⓑ tip This type of concrete mix, which contains no large gravel aggregate, is more delicate than the premixed kind. It works better in a sand mold, because gravel aggregate would be forced into the sand and show on the surface of the finished product. Using no aggregate produces a look more like sandstone. It's not strong when freshly unmolded, though, and must be treated carefully until it's had a chance to cure.

Step 4: Remove the Mold

Let the concrete set for 24 to 48 hours, then remove the screws from the sides of the mold and pull it away from the cast sluice. Rinse the sand free from the concrete with water to reveal the surface. Roughen any surfaces that look too smooth with a wire brush. Cover it with damp paper towels and plastic for a three-day curing period.

Making the Hypertufa Trough

Step 1: Mix the Hypertufa

In a 1-quart (1 l) yogurt container mix:
- 2 parts sifted peat
- 2 parts mason's sand
- 1 part Portland cement

When the dry ingredients are thoroughly blended, add just enough water to thoroughly moisten the mix. It should be just wet enough to hold together when squeezed, but with no extra water.

> **tip** You can also cast the hypertufa over a plywood box to produce a trough of any dimension you need — it will simply result in a heavier reservoir.

Step 2: Apply the Hypertufa to the Styrofoam Box

Turn the box over and brush a coat of yellow glue on the bottom as well as the bottom few inches of the sides. Immediately begin applying the hypertufa mixture to the surface, about ½ to ¾ inch (13 to 19 mm) thick. Smooth it with a mason's trowel to produce a fairly flat, stonelike surface. Any edge marks from the trowel will add to the look of cut stone.

Allow this section to dry overnight. Then coat the sides and top edge the next day. For your last application, cover the entire inside of the box. This should result in a stone trough about 2 inches (5 cm) thick overall. ▼

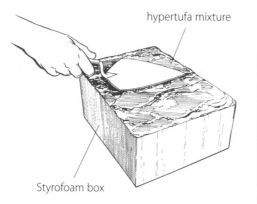

hypertufa mixture

Styrofoam box

▶ Upon close examination, you can see the rough, pitted surface that hypertufa creates.

Step 3: Cure the Hypertufa

Allow the hypertufa-covered trough to sit undisturbed for several days. To encourage mossy growth over time, once it has hardened you can leave it outside (as long as it's not freezing) to neutralize. Cement is alkaline and will be neutralized by the acidity of rain falling through the branches of acidic plants such as evergreens. When the trough has had a few weeks to cure, it's ready for use.

Building the Fountain

▶ Step 1: Build the Base of the Retaining Wall

The easiest way to build a retaining wall is to cut a level terrace into a slope, leaving a vertical wall. You then use stone to retain this wall against erosion. The soil is packed behind the stones, supporting them and keeping them in place. The fit of the stones doesn't have to be tight enough to hold the wall up by itself, and the wall doesn't have to be vertical — most of the taller ones lean back toward the earth being retained.

As you assemble stones and pack dirt behind them, make sure your wall is going to be high enough to clear the top of your trough.

Embed plants along the top of the retaining wall to make it seem a part of the natural landscape.

▶ Step 2: Embed the Vinyl Hose and Concrete Sluice

As you reach the top of the wall, and before you place the concrete sluice, you need to embed in the wall a length of old garden hose through which you can run the vinyl tubing, from the trough to the pump. Be sure it's a loose fit, so in the event of ice damage, you'll be able to pull a piece of new vinyl through. Then embed the garden hose and the vinyl tubing together in the soil and stone as you build the wall. Set the concrete sluice into place high enough to clear the wood or stone trough. Bend the vinyl tubing so that it discharges onto the sluice, and finish off the wall while making sure that the sluice emerges from beneath a nice flat capstone to hide the tubing. ▼

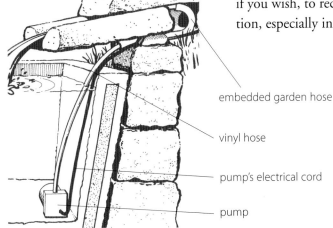

embedded garden hose

vinyl hose

pump's electrical cord

pump

▶ Step 3: Test the Water Flow

Set the pump in the trough, fill the trough with water, and trim the vinyl hose to length and plug it into the pump. Then plug the pump into a GFCI outlet and observe the flow of water from your sluice into the trough. If the water flows too hard or not hard enough, adjust the pump's flow control. This fountain is at its best running very gently, even dripping.

▶ Step 4: Add Plants

The stones of the wall can be encouraged to accumulate moss, ferns can be planted in the soil pockets, and ivy can hang over the top edge. Marginal bog plants such as pickerelweed and cattails can be set to stand proudly in the trough. Encourage the whole fountain, if you wish, to recede into the vegetation, especially in a shady location.

Small Ceramic Spouting Sculpture

This project gives you the opportunity to design and create an original piece of clay sculpture — in this case, a frog — and insert a tube within it to carry water from a pump. As an outdoor fountain, it uses a simple preformed plastic pool, available in many garden supply stores, buried in your garden. (You can adapt the project for indoors by making the sculpture smaller and using a large bowl for a tabletop fountain.) In this example we'll create a bullfrog about 6 inches (15 cm) high in a small pool about 24 inches (60 cm) in diameter. This fountain is easy to fit into the smallest garden and, at 8 inches (20 cm) deep, is virtually child-safe.

Return to Working with Clay on page 79 to review the requirements for ceramic sculpture. You will need access to a kiln, and you should create your frog sculpture from clay that will fire to maturity in the kiln you plan to use.

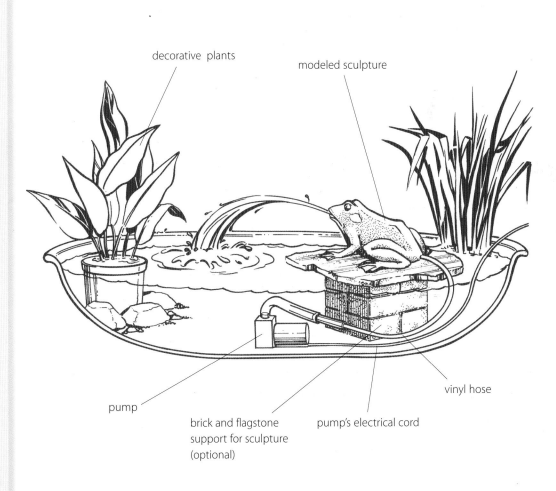

decorative plants

modeled sculpture

pump

brick and flagstone support for sculpture (optional)

pump's electrical cord

vinyl hose

MATERIALS

For the Reservoir
• Preformed plastic pool, about 24" in diameter x 8" deep (60 cm x 20 cm)

For the Pump
• Pump, 80–140 GPH (304–532 l per hour)
• GFCI outlet or extension cord

Fountain Elements
• 5–6 pounds (2.3–2.7 kg) clay
• 1/8" (3 mm) ID clear vinyl hose: 12" (30 cm)
• 1/4" and 3/4" (6 and 9 mm) ID vinyl hose: 12" (30 cm) each (to adapt the 1/8", or 3 mm, hose to the pump's outflow)

Tools
• Sculpture stand or lazy Susan
• Clay-modeling tools
• Paper towels
• Several sheets of lightweight plastic, such as the kind dry cleaning is wrapped in
• Silicone caulk , small tube

If you don't have the time or inclination to make your own spouting sculpture, you can often purchase one from a local garden center. They come in all shapes and sizes.

Studying the Natural Form

Whenever you attempt to imitate Mother Nature, it's helpful to study her work carefully. The bullfrog you'll create here is intended to be as faithful a portrait of the real thing as you can make. The library and children's bookstores are good resources for photographs of bullfrogs in different positions. I recommend photocopying these for constant reference while you sculpt. Once you have collected and studied reference material, sit down in front of your sculpture stand and begin!

Be patient as you endeavor to translate the two-dimensional photos into a three-dimensional work. It takes a lot of time and persistence. The benefits of all this work include an increased ability to see shapes accurately, and an increased respect for the beauty of natural forms. If it takes you more than one modeling session to create a form that pleases you, just remember to cover the clay tightly with damp paper towels and plastic to keep it soft between sessions. Feel free to experiment — by adding and removing clay, you will begin to reveal the form you are seeking.

Creating the Clay Sculpture

▶ Step 1: Model the Frog from Clay

Pat a lump of clay into the shape of the frog's body, then attach thick bent coils for the hind legs. In the initial phase of forming the sculpture, embed the ⅛-inch (3 mm) ID vinyl hose in the clay, to form a channel that will lead water from the pump to the frog's mouth. Wrap it in several layers of soft plastic before embedding it in the sculpture so that, when finished, you will be able to pull it out of the hardening clay. Rather than letting the hose protrude from the frog's mouth, hold it back about ¼ inch (6 mm) and simply model a small hole between the frog's lips to connect with the hose inside. The other end of the hose should exit from the bottom of the sculpture. Carve clay from the inside of thick areas, like the main body of the frog, so that the clay is nowhere thicker than an inch (2.5 cm) or so. This will make drying far safer. ▼

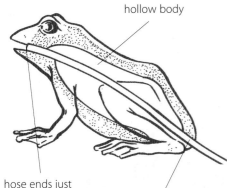

hollow body

hose ends just short of mouth

vinyl hose

▶ Step 2: Dry the Frog Sculpture

When the frog is finished, begin to let it dry slowly. The clay will shrink as it dries, and it's apt to crack in the thickest areas. Drying very slowly over a period of several weeks is the best insurance against this. Keep the sculpture wrapped in plastic while allowing the paper towels to dry out. When the clay has hardened slightly, remove the vinyl hose tubing and its wrappings from the inside of the sculpture.

▶ Step 3: Fire the Sculpture

When the clay has been bone dry for several weeks (no coolness to the touch), it is safe to fire. To be absolutely safe, placing the dry sculpture piece in a cool oven (150°F, or 66°C) for several hours is a good added precaution. The reason for all this care is that any residual moisture will vaporize in the kiln. Water expands to 1,700 times its liquid volume when it vaporizes. When this happens in a piece of clay sculpture, chips of clay fly in all directions, destroying not only your work but sometimes that of other artists as well. So, after all precautions have been taken, bring your sculpture to the kiln and fire it to the correct temperature for the clay body you have chosen.

Setting Up Your Fountain

▶ Step 1: Attach the Tubing to the Frog

Reinstall the ⅛-inch (3 mm) hose inside the frog's body. It does not need to reach the point where it ended before firing, because the clay channel will carry the water to the frog's mouth. Simply squeeze some silicone caulk onto its sides and force the tubing into the channel. Push it as far as it will go easily. Add more silicone to caulk it firmly into the hole and allow this assembly to dry.

▶ Step 2: Test the Water Flow

Bury the preformed pool in your garden near a GFCI outlet. Set the pump in the pool and fill the pool with water. Place the frog in the pool or at its edge, then connect the hose to the pump's outflow, telescoping smaller sections as necessary. Adjust the lengths until the tubing reaches comfortably from the pump to the frog. Now plug in the pump and adjust the flow control until the water stream is as you wish, the frog is sitting in a prominent location, and the sound of the water is audible and relaxing. Remember that sound and splash always go together. If your fountain splashes water outside the pool, it will require frequent filling. Move the frog and adjust the flow control on the pump until the flow is optimal. Then decorate the edges of the pool with stones and plantings as desired.

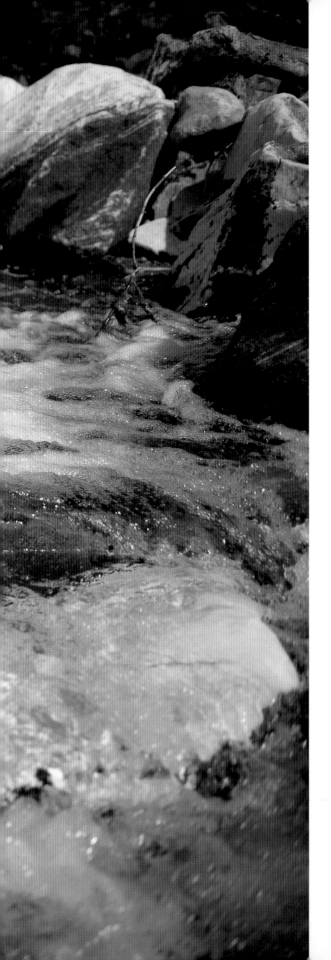

5 Building a Full-Sized Waterfall

A waterfall and pond are perhaps the most satisfying of all fountain projects because, more than any others, they closely imitate nature. With enough skill and energy, we can even create an environment where aquatic animals can reside in prolific health. Seeing them reproduce in their enthusiastic fashion is cheering to the spirit. It gives us hope to see how rapidly nature accepts a sensitively managed offering of habitat. As we enjoy the added attraction of a garden pond, we are sure to gain an increased appreciation of natural systems.

Fascinated by the added dimension of water in the garden, Barnabas Webster spends most of his waking moments designing and installing water garden features for a growing list of clients. Named for the sacred lotus, his company, Nelumbo Water Gardens (see appendix C) provides everything from excavation plans to frogs, cattails, and ongoing maintenance. The following project gives you Barney's recipe for a small pond and waterfall that you can construct without heavy equipment.

Small Waterfall and Pond

his project, designed by Barnabas Webster of Nelumbo Water Gardens, creates an outdoor pond with a small waterfall about 3 feet (1 m) high that you can construct without heavy equipment. You will need an area of garden at least 4 feet by 8 feet (1.2 by 2.4 m) in order to construct the minimal-sized pool, 3 by 3 (1 m by 1 m), with the adjacent waterfall and surrounding bog area. If you have a sloping site, so much the better.

Barney uses a water-hyacinth biofilter in his ponds, and he locates it in the waterfall. Any waterfall — small or large — can accommodate the system he has developed, and his ponds all boast amazingly clear water because of it. His filters usually need cleaning only once a year, even with surprisingly large populations of fish and (even messier) turtles living in the ponds.

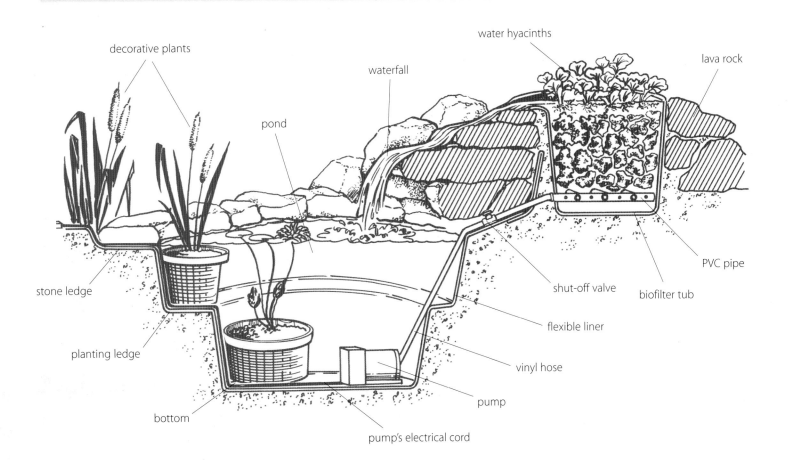

decorative plants

water hyacinths

lava rock

waterfall

pond

PVC pipe

stone ledge

shut-off valve

biofilter tub

planting ledge

flexible liner

vinyl hose

bottom

pump

pump's electrical cord

MATERIALS

For the Pond and Streambed
- Vinyl hose: 10' (3 m) each of 1" (2.5 cm) ID hose and a smaller hose, sized to fit pump's outflow
- Flexible liner (45-mil EPDM is best)
- Carpet scraps or liner underlayment
- Builder's sand, pea gravel: about 250 pounds (114 kg) each for 100-gallon (380 l) pond
- Ample supply of building stone

For the Biofilter
- Preformed biofilter tub
- PVC pipe: 10' (3 m) length of 1" (2.5 cm) ID pipe
- 3 four-way connectors for PVC pipe
- 7 end caps for PVC pipe
- 3 hose clamps
- 50 pounds (22.7 kg) broken lava rock
- Several water hyacinth plants

For the Pump
- Pump: Size and power will depend on the size of your waterfall; review The Pump and Electrical System on page 4
- GFCI outdoor outlet or GFCI extension cord buried in PVC pipe
- 1 in-line shut-off valve

Tools
- Spade, wheelbarrow, crowbar, strong back
- Pipe cement and saw
- Electric drill with 3/16" (5 mm) drill bit

Consider stocking your pond with small fish; larger ponds can hold koi (shown here). If you live in colder regions, check with your local extension service to determine how deep the pond should be to allow the fish to safely winter over.

Finding the Right Stones

You will need a supply of stone to form the waterfall and line the edges of the pond. You can collect stone if you have access to rocky land, or buy it from a landscape stone company. The latter can probably offer stone in several types. Softly rounded, irregularly shaped fieldstones will create the look of a natural, weathered streambed. Sometimes the stones will already have lichens and moss clinging to them. Such stones are highly prized by Japanese garden designers and require a fairly humid climate to flourish.

Estimate the amount of stones you'll need by considering the volume of your waterfall and stone ledge. Buy more than you need, so that you will be able to pick and choose. Stone is typically sold by the cubic yard and can be delivered by the supplier.

Planning the Waterfall and Pond

▶ Step 1: Site the Pond and Waterfall

As you plan the layout, a rope or garden hose can be useful for marking the undulating edge you envision for the pond. If you have a natural drop in elevation, site the elements accordingly, with the waterfall rising from the highest ground. Try not to place your pond in a gully, where run-off will flow into it, bringing in pollution from lawn fertilizers, not to mention overfilling the pond and allowing escape of your fish into the garden! If possible, avoid areas beneath large trees, where heavy shade will reduce your choices of flowering plants.

▶ Step 2: Calculate the Water Volume

It's important to make the pond large enough in relation to the waterfall so that when you start the pump and fill the streambed from the pond, the drop in water level is not too drastic. By calculating the volume of the waterfall and then of the pond, you can estimate the drop in waterline that will occur.

Calculate volume by multiplying length by width by depth to give you the cubic volume of water in your pond. If you're measuring in feet, multiply this number by 7.5 to yield the number of gallons in the pond. If you're measuring in meters, multiply this number by 1,000 to yield the number of liters. Do the same for the streambed that will form your waterfall.

For Example: Your pond measures 3 feet wide by 4 feet long by 2 feet deep. To allow for the rounded corners, call the pond 2.5 by 3.5 by 1.5 feet. Multiplying these gives you a total of 13.125 cubic feet. Multiply this by 7.5 gallons per cubic foot to reach a figure of 98.44 or, roughly, 100 gallons.

The waterfall is 3 feet high and at the spillway (the point at which falling water begins) it's 1 inch deep and 4 inches wide. Following the same formula, 1 x 4 x 36 = 144 cubic inches or 1 cubic foot; multiply this by 7.5 gallons per cubic foot to reach a figure of roughly 7½ gallons. The waterfall should thus reduce the pond's depth by about 8 percent — less than 2 inches.

▶ Step 3: Plan for Access to Water and Electricity

Another consideration is your pond's proximity to a water supply (for easy filling) and to electrical service. You can have a licensed electrician run a separate circuit from your electrical panel to an outdoor outlet with a GFCI, or purchase an extension cord already equipped with a GFCI and run it from a house outlet. Wherever the cord crosses a walkway or lawn, bury a piece of 2-inch (5 cm) PVC pipe and run the cord through. When you're winterizing the pond, you can remove the cord for storage.

Excavating the Pond

▶ Step 1: Level a Site for the Pond

If your site is not level, you will need to either build up the downhill edge of the pond or cut away its uphill edge, forming a small cliff that you can cover with stone for the waterfall. Use a level on a long board to plan the location of the waterline on this surface while digging.

> **ⓑ tip** If you don't have a small hill on which to site the waterfall, build one from the material you dig out of the pond site. As you dig out the pond, transport the material to the site you've chosen for the elevation and reposition it there, packing it down firmly.

▶ Step 2: Dig Out the Stone Ledge

The pond descends in a series of ledges. The first surrounds the edge and contains the stones and plants that conceal the edge of the liner. Use a level as you dig it to make sure it's broad, level, and uniformly 2 to 3 inches (5 to 7.5 cm) deeper than the waterline. Design the stones you'll place on the ledge to vary in width. Wide pockets — where water barely reaches the soil, keeping it wet but not flooded — can be planted as bog gardens. Some of the showiest flowering plants, such as irises and cardinal flowers, require precisely these conditions. The stones should sit firmly enough for you to stand on.

Constructing the Biofilter

▶ Step 3: Dig Out the Planting Ledge

The pond wall should now drop almost vertically about 10 inches (25 cm) to the next ledge, which should be as wide and level as you can afford. Most of the aquatic plants you'll use do best sitting in individual pots on this ledge. This second ledge also serves as a safety feature, offering a secure step to anyone climbing out of the pond.

▶ Step 4: Dig Out the Bottom

In colder regions, check with your local extension service to find out how deep the pond needs to be so that fish and frogs can hibernate safely over the winter. Two feet (60 cm) is plenty in most areas. Make the walls drop vertically from the plant ledge to the bottom to allow for maximum water volume; the best protection you can offer animal residents is high water quality, which is far easier to maintain where there is adequate water volume.

After a season of use, the pond will accumulate a layer of mud and debris in the bottom. This is an important refuge for hibernating frogs and fish, so allow a little extra room for this layer. ▼

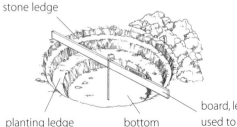

stone ledge

planting ledge   bottom   board, level, and measuring tape used to keep the ledges level

▶ Step 1: Assemble the Biofilter

Biofilter tubs come in black plastic, about 15 gallons (57 l) in size, with a wide molded spout to form the spillway for your waterfall and an inlet fitting in the bottom. Plan the grid of PVC pipe so that it will fit inside the biofilter tub. Use the four-way connectors to form three arms, as shown, and cap each end. With an electric drill, bore a sequence of holes through the top of the pipes. Place the grid inside the tub, on the bottom, and attach it to the inlet fitting. Rather than having water rush into the tub in a solid stream at the point of the inlet, the PVC grid diffuses the dirty inlet water, creating a better filter. On top of the PVC grid, fill the tub almost to the top with broken chunks of lava rock. ▼

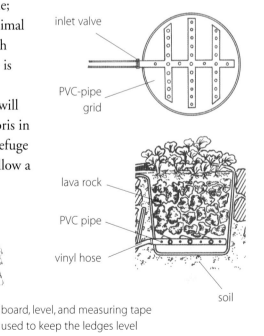

inlet valve

PVC-pipe grid

lava rock

PVC pipe

vinyl hose

soil

▶ Step 2: Set the Biofilter

Dig a hole for the biofilter tub (or set the tub on the pile of fill you have removed from the pond) and adjust the height of its spillway to around 3 feet (1 m) above the pond's surface. With a hose clamp, attach a length of vinyl hose to the inlet valve and run this down into the pond. Pack a layer of soil around the tub — eventually you'll tuck the edge of the pond liner against the soil, behind the rocks that form the spillway. Let the hose to the tub's inlet come out of the soil at a point several inches above the pond's water level. ▼

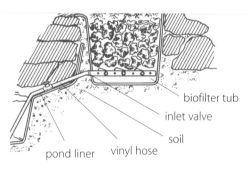

biofilter tub

inlet valve

soil

pond liner   vinyl hose

Why Lava Rock?

Nitrifying bacteria will naturally colonize the nooks and crannies of lava rock's enormous surface area. These bacteria convert the toxic ammonia of fish waste into relatively harmless nitrates, which are consumed by the mat of water hyacinths that you'll plant in the upper few inches of the biofilter tub.

Finishing the Pond

▶ Step 1: Size the Liner

When you are sure of the size and shape of your pond and waterfall, buy a liner sized as follows: Measure the footprint of your water feature, including stone ledge, pond, and waterfall, yielding a rectangle expressed in length by width. Add to this figure depth times 2. Then add 2 extra feet (60 cm) so that there will be a foot (30 cm) of extra liner all the way around.

If the waterfall is short enough to include in this calculation, you can cover the whole system with one sheet of liner, thus avoiding joints that could potentially leak. But the elevation inherent in the waterfall makes it possible to use a scrap of liner for it, running the pond liner up underneath it for a 12 inch (30 cm) overlap. This overlap must be located in a drop where water does not pool, so as to avoid leaks.

For Example: Let's return to our pond that's 3 feet wide by 4 feet long and 2 feet deep. It has planting ledges all around, and a 3-foot waterfall that's 6 inches wide.

Width (3') plus 2 × depth (2' × 2) = 7' wide, plus 2 × stone ledges (1' × 2) = 9'.

Length (4') plus 2 × depth (2' × 2) = 8' wide, plus 2 × stone ledges (1' × 2) = 10'.

Conclusion: If you buy a liner 10 feet by 12 feet, you will have a scrap for the waterfall at least 3 feet wide cut from one of its sides.

▶ Step 2: Pad and Install the Liner

You can use a supply of old carpet scraps or buy liner underlayment (a fibrous pad sold by pond supply companies) to cushion the liner. This prevents pointed stones and roots from piercing it under the stretching force of water pressure. Use a layer of builder's sand to fill dips in the excavation, smoothing the surface before the carpet is laid in. Finally, lay the liner in the pond while filling it with water to force it into every crevice. Let it lie on the ground untrimmed as long as possible — this makes it easier for you to make changes later. Lift the liner up the waterfall face and, well above water level, make a small hole in the rubber liner. Pull the vinyl hose from the biofilter through so that it can be run down to the pump in the pond. This hole should be located where water does not run directly onto it; your goal is the air space beneath the large overhanging stone.

Building the Waterfall

▶ Step 1: Install the Pump

Set the flow control of the pump all the way to high, since you'll be installing a shut-off valve in the line, and place it in the pond. Plug it into a GFCI outlet, or an extension cord fitted with a GFCI, as previously described

▶ Step 2: Set the Base Stones and Shut-Off Valve

Begin building the waterfall by setting fairly large, stable stones in the stone ledge at its base. Leave room at the side of the waterfall for a small chamber in the stone ledge, hidden by a covering stone lid, through which the vinyl hose connecting the pump to the biofilter tub can run. Inside the hidden chamber, install a shut-off valve in the vinyl hose. This makes controlling the pump's flow easier and offers a good place for reducing the size of the tubing, which is usually larger at the biofilter inlet than at the pump outflow. (Hardware stores sell a selection of PVC fittings that you can attach to the valve to reduce the size of the line.) Then attach the hose to the pump's outflow.

Step 3: Build the Overhang

Build up the front of the waterfall by setting stones over the liner covering the biofilter, allowing for an overhanging ledge where water falls 6 to 12 inches (15 to 30 cm) into the pond. This will greatly amplify the sound of the water, as well as providing an air space for any necessary breaks in the liner (such as the hole for the hose to the biofilter or possibly the overlap in liners between waterfall and pond). Continue to stack stone up the front of the biofilter until the liner is held firmly in place beneath the spillway. ▼

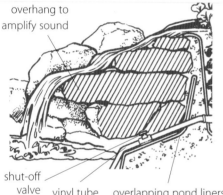

overhang to amplify sound

shut-off valve   vinyl tube   overlapping pond liners

Step 4: Test the Water Flow

At this point check your waterfall with water. This is a good chance to test your pump, although a garden hose will work just as well. Fill the biofilter to overflowing and let the water run over the stones you have placed beneath the spillway. If you begin to overfill the pond liner, you can always siphon out some water.

Finishing Touches

Step 1: Tuck the Liner

Bring the edge of the liner to the surface beside the waterfall stones, cupping the stream of water on both sides. Making sure that none of the stream escapes around it, fold back at least 6 inches (15 cm) of untrimmed edge to hide beneath stones arranged around the sides and, if necessary, the back of the earth mound. Trim the extra from the liner around the pond, leaving 6 inches (15 cm) for tucking underneath as you backfill up to the edge stones.

Step 2: Plant the Biofilter and Pond

Set the water hyacinths in the top layer of the biofilter tub. They are floating plants and will happily thrive in the ever-flowing water. Note that they are not winter-hardy and do not winter well indoors. If you live in colder areas, you may have to discard your plants at the end of the growing season and purchase more in the spring. In warmer regions, make sure that the plants are well contained in the tub, as water hyacinths are extremely invasive and will spread quickly.

You are now ready to finish the margin of the pond. Fill the shallow stone ledge with gravel, clumps of marginal bog plants, and stones left from the streambed construction. You can bury the cord from the pump in this ledge, too. See appendix B for planting suggestions.

Draining the Pond with a Siphon

This is a very handy technique to learn, and you can use it later as well if the pond needs to be emptied for cleaning. Connect a garden hose to a faucet and drop the other end in the pond. Turn on the water, and when the hose is filled with water and begins spilling into the pond, quickly turn off the water while simultaneously crimping the faucet end of the hose shut. With the hose full of water and one end still in the pond, unscrew it from the faucet. Carry this end to an area of lower elevation than the pond and release the crimp. Water should run from the hose, draining the pond. It will continue to do so as long as the other end remains beneath the surface of the pond water.

▶ This waterfall is set over a fairly large pond. The mass of water hyacinths forming the top layer of the biofilter create a vivid green accent.

Appendix A: Bringing Life to Your Fountain

Nowhere is nature's determination to create and support life displayed with more stubborn persistence than in a watery setting. Even the smallest indoor fountain can become an aquatic ecosystem if you fill it with suitable plants and allow it to function undisturbed. The amount of light available is often key, as is the oxygen level of the water, enhanced by the falling and bubbling produced by the fountain itself.

A successful garden pond must contain both plants and animals for a healthy balance. Photosynthesis, the system by which plants produce food from sunlight, produces oxygen and requires carbon dioxide. Fish and other water-breathing animals use up the oxygen and produce carbon dioxide. The nitrogen cycle is another hallowed example of the synergy between plants and animals: Animal waste is made up mostly of ammonia. This is converted by the ubiquitous nitrifying bacteria into nitrites, and finally into nitrates — fertilizer, or food for plants. As the plants flourish in the presence of nitrates, they are eaten by the animals, resulting in the excretion of more waste, completing the cycle.

Whenever you create an environment as complex as an outdoor wetland, it is best to tread with respect, stocking plants and animals native to your region whenever possible. Native animals and plants will survive local temperature extremes without protection, and they'll respond to a range of subtle controls of which we are only dimly aware. If yours is a tropical climate where winter frost doesn't provide a natural control for tropical plants and animals that escape from your garden into the wild, be especially careful. Water hyacinth, for instance, is an invasive import that is safe to introduce only into colder climates where it can never spread to the wild, choking waterways as it does in parts of the southeastern United States. And loosestrife, attractive for its magenta spikes in late summer, is an invasive plant impervious to frost. Whole ecosystems in the Northeast have been permanently altered by its introduction.

Following are lists of common plants for water gardens, and the situations in which they best function or thrive. For more detail on how to propagate and care for the plants, as well as how to choose among them, consult a water gardening book, or look for a local garden center that specializes in water gardening, and ask for advice there.

There are many more choices than those listed here, of course. Use these lists as a beginning guide, then go out and explore the options available to you in your region and climate.

Ferns, Mosses, and Lichens

Mosses and ferns, while they must be rooted in soil above water level, love the moisture associated with water gardens. The variety of bright greens available in mosses and the strong, serrated leaf shapes of all ferns add immeasurably to the design of a large or small fountain. They may be found among the rocks in moist woodlands. Using these rocks around your fountain brings the added bonus of the lichen's unique gray-green coloration and flat, peeling texture. Ferns are also easy to find in most garden centers. If you use these plants in indoor fountains, keep them misted for best results.

Definitions

When you walk into a garden center to purchase plants for your fountain or pond, these are the terms you'll need to know.

Potted: Needs to be rooted in soil in a pot; the pot can then be placed in the pool of water.

Marginal: Grows in shallow water, with its leaves extended out of or floating on the water.

Floating: Grows without soil, floating freely in the water.

Oxygenator: Diffuses oxygen into the water.

Submerged Oxygenators

Oxygenators diffuse oxygen into the water, a necessary element for animal life. An incidental advantage to submerged oxygenators is that they provide cover and habitat for the smallest fishes and tadpoles. Goldfish lay eggs on submerged stems and leaves, and are more likely to breed in ponds with plenty of submerged plants.

- Anacharis (*Egeria densa*) — some times sold as *Elodea*
- Cabomba (*Cabomba caroliniana*)
- Hair grass (*Eleocharis acicularis*)
- Hygrophilla (*Hygrophilla polysperma*)
- Parrot's feather (*Myriophyllum aquaticum*)
- Sagittaria (*Sagittaria graminea*)
- Vallisneria (*Vallisneria gigantea*)

Plants with Showy Flowers

If you have a pond or large reservoir and want to show off some beautiful blooms, there are many aquatic plants with large, vibrant, showy flowers to choose from, including:

- Blue flag (*Iris versicolor*)
- Cardinal flower (*Lobelia cardinalis*)
- Imperial taro (*Colocasia esculenta*)
- Lotus (*Nelumbo* spp.)
- Pickerelweed (*Pontederia cordata*)
- Water canna (*Thalia geniculata*)
- Water hyacinth (*Eichhornia crassipes*)
- Water lily (*Nymphaea* spp.)
- Yellow flag (*Iris pseudacorus*)

Plants for Small, Indoor Fountains

Small, shade-tolerant plants are probably the most useful to the indoor fountaineer. Many of these trusty individuals will survive in tiny pools under office lighting. My favorite varieties are:

- Acorus (*Acorus calamus, A. gramineus*)
- Duckweed (*Lemna minor*)
- Dwarf papyrus (*Cyperus haspan*)
- Dwarf umbrella palm (*Cyperus alternifolius*)
- Salvinia (*Salvinia auriculata*)

Plants for Large, Sunny Reservoirs

If your pond or large reservoir receives heavy sun exposure, these are the plants to try. Keep in mind that although these plants thrive in full sun, many of them will do just as well in partial shade.

- Arrowhead arum (*Sagittaria latifolia*)
- Blue flag (*Iris versicolor*)
- Cardinal flower (*Lobelia cardinalis*)
- Cattail (*Typha* spp.)
- Imperial taro (*Colocasia esculenta*)
- Lotus (*Nelumbo* spp.)
- Pickerelweed (*Pontederia cordata*)
- Water canna (*Thalia geniculata*)
- Water hawthorne (*Aponogeton distachyus*)
- Water lily (*Nymphaea* spp.)
- Water plantain (*Alisma plantago-aquatica*)
- Yellow flag (*Iris pseudacorus*)

Common Animals for Water Gardens

Aquatic animals are available in pet stores, from pond supply catalogs, and in the wild. Some are protected by law; others are as common as ditch water in spring and can be collected for the asking. Some will remain in your pond when you introduce them, some will stroll off into the woods, and some will arrive uninvited.

Aside from the obvious entertainment value of having animals live in your pond, some can have a noticeable environmental impact. Turtles and fish, especially large and greedy fish like koi and big goldfish, excrete large amounts of solid waste. This requires large populations of nitrifying bacteria to control the potentially toxic ammonia levels, and uses lots of dissolved oxygen. If you have these animals in your pond, be sure to pump the water through a biofilter to treat it with nitrifying bacteria and increase its oxygen level.

Some animals, such as snails and tadpoles, consume algae and thus keep the pond looking tidy. Others, such as freshwater mussels, filter pond water through their bodies and remove organic material such as fish waste and rotting leaves, resulting in improved water quality. Even the smallest goldfish gobble up mosquito larvae to keep the pond from contributing this pest to your garden. Some plants, such as cattails and water hyacinth, are also excellent water purifiers.

Although more exotic animals such as fire newts and African tree frogs can be purchased from suppliers, it usually works best to respect the species native to your area. At best, exotics will perish in temperature extremes for which they are not suited. At worst, they will escape from your garden to flourish unchecked by natural predators, to upset the balance in the world outside your gates.

Appendix B: Maintenance

For the most part garden ponds and fountains offer a carefree alternative to high-maintenance conventional gardens. There's no need to weed, as weeds form the backbone of aquatic life. No need to water, beyond the occasional refilling — which usually manages itself while you admire your shining fish and delicate water lilies. No need to be a neatnik about cleaning it out, because it's healthier with a layer of muck in the bottom.

Cleaning Fountains and Ponds

Providers of pond supplies offer a range of ultraviolet filters, skimmers, and water treatment products ranging from natural nitrifying bacteria to a dark blue dye designed to retard the growth of algae by restricting sunlight. Usually the simplest approach is best. Let nature take its course before you assume you need to interfere by introducing man-made products.

Many people have asked me whether there is any product available to keep fountains sparkling clean without effort. Chlorine bleach, added in minute amounts to water, kills bacteria. One drop of bleach per pint (0.5 l) of water is drinkable and should kill the bacteria that cause slime in fountains. Larger amounts may attack plastic pump parts, causing other problems. Still, since many fountains contain plants and the small snails and other water animals that accompany them, it's probably best not to add any chemicals, including bleach, to the water. A better alternative is to let your plants do the work. Their roots spread throughout the small pool, purifying the water. However, if you're without plants, simply wash the fountain parts every month or so.

If your area is supplied by hard water, which can leave deposits of mineral salts on fountain parts, use distilled water in the fountain. If you're unable to use distilled water, salt deposits often can be dissolved if soaked in vinegar.

Winterizing

Winterizing fountains and ponds for freezing temperatures is a matter of simple common sense. Estimate the depth to which your pond will freeze. Anything within this zone that can be damaged by the expansion of ice should be removed, emptied, washed, and stored until spring. A submerged pump may be removed and thoroughly cleaned to remove any algae. Frost-tender tropical plants and animals can winter in an indoor aquarium, water-filled tub, or even a bowl on a windowsill. Hardy plants and goldfish can be left in ponds for the winter with one stipulation: Goldfish, frogs, and turtles require water sufficiently deep to provide an ice-free zone for hibernation.

Maintenance for Ponds

If your fountain flows into a pond, you should know that ponds do require some care, but very little compared to dry-land gardens. Hardy plants will go dormant in winter, leaving a layer of dying vegetation that uses oxygen to decompose. This competes with the needs of fish, which depend on a fairly high level of dissolved oxygen for survival. At some point before spring warms the water to a comfortable level, you need to remove the decomposing vegetation. If possible, first cut it back in late summer, when lingering hot afternoons make this muddy wallow a pleasure. Then as soon as you can stand to get into the water in spring, remove leaves from the bottom by simply scooping them out in handfuls. Be careful to examine these shapeless blobs before you add them to the compost pile — sometimes only the slightest movement will alert you to the fact that this is a hibernating bullfrog, still too cold to respond to your touch!

Draining a pond and scrubbing the algae and bacteria from the pond liner is not the good housekeeping it seems. These inhabitants of your aquatic environment perform countless services of which our understanding is only slowly developing. A good rule when maintaining your pond is, "If it ain't broke, don't fix it!"

If your pond has a biofilter with pipes and lava rocks, clean this with a garden hose to remove accumulated fish waste. Store any plumbing for the winter after being sure all water is drained from it.

Appendix C: Mail-Order Suppliers

If local sources don't exist or don't have what you want, you can order aquatic plants and fountains parts (and sometimes the whole fountain!) from the companies listed below. Contact them for catalogs and price lists.

Adams and Adkins, Inc., 104 South Early Street, Alexandria, VA 22304, (703) 823-3404, Fax (703) 823-5367, Web site: www.adamsandadkins.com. *Fountain supplies and complete fountains.*

The Brass Baron, 10151 Pacific Mesa Boulevard, Suite 104, San Diego, CA 92121, Web site: www.brassbaron.com. *Cast bronze statuary and decorative fiberglass pools; wholesale only, but their web site has a dealer directory.*

Frank's Cane and Rush Supply, 7252 Heil Avenue, Huntington Beach, CA 92647, (714) 847-0707, Web site: www.franksupply.com. *Chair cane for weaving, bamboo spouts, and bamboo poles.*

Harry's Special Places, 20489 Denby, Redford, MI 48240, (313) 531-2212, Fax (313) 531-2213. *Water garden, fountain, and pond supplies.*

Hughes Water Gardens, 25289 SW Stafford Road, Tualatin, OR 97062, (503) 638-1709, Fax (503) 638-9035, Web site: www.waterplant.com. *Water garden, fountain, and pond supplies.*

Lilypons Water Gardens, 6800 Lilypons Road, P.O. Box 10, Buckystown, MD 21717, (800) 723-7667, Web site: www.lilypons.com. *Water garden, fountain, and pond supplies.*

Nelumbo Water Gardens (Barnabas Webster), 44 Collation Circle, North Kingstown, RI 02852, (401) 294-3717. *In the region, water feature installation and maintenance; provides everything from backhoe and grading plan to frogs, cattails, and ongoing maintenance.*

Maryland Aquatic Nurseries, Inc., 3427 North Furnace Road, Jarrettsville, MD 21084, (410) 557-7615, Fax (410) 692-2837, Web site: www.MarylandAquatic.com. *Water garden, fountain, and pond supplies.*

Paradise Water Gardens, 14 May Street, Whitman, MA 02382, (800) 955-0161, Fax (781) 447-4591, Web site: www.paradisewatergardens.com. *Water garden, fountain, and pond supplies.*

Real Goods, 555 Leslie Street, Ukiah, CA 95482-5526, Fax (800) 508-2342, Web site: www.realgoods.com. *Solar powered fountain pumps.*

Reimer Waterscapes, 55653 Bestline, RR#3, Tillsonburg, ON N4G 4H3, (519) 842-6049, Fax (519) 688-5459. *Water garden, fountain, and pond supplies.*

Slocum Water Gardens, 1101 Cypress Gardens Boulevard, Winter Haven, FL 33884-1932, (941) 293-7151. *Water garden, fountain, and pond supplies.*

Van Ness Water Gardens, 2460 North Euclid Avenue, Upland, CA 91784-1199, (800) 205-2425, Fax (909) 949-7217, Web site: www.vnwg.com. *Water garden, fountain, and pond supplies.*

Waterford Gardens, 74 East Allendale Road, Saddle River, NJ 07458, (201) 327-0721, Fax (201) 327-0684, Web site: waterford-gardens.com. *Water garden, fountain, and pond supplies.*

Wicklein's Water Gardens, P.O. Box 9780, Baldwin, MD 21013, (800) 382-6716, Web site: www.wickleinaquatics.com. *Water garden, fountain, and pond supplies.*

Index

Page references in *italics* indicate illustrations; those in **bold** indicate charts.